Mentality and Freedom

Mentality and Freedom

Achieve Internal Freedom Through Mentality, Mental Habits Autonomy, and Timeless Mindset Freedom.

(Illustrated, Refined & Edited)

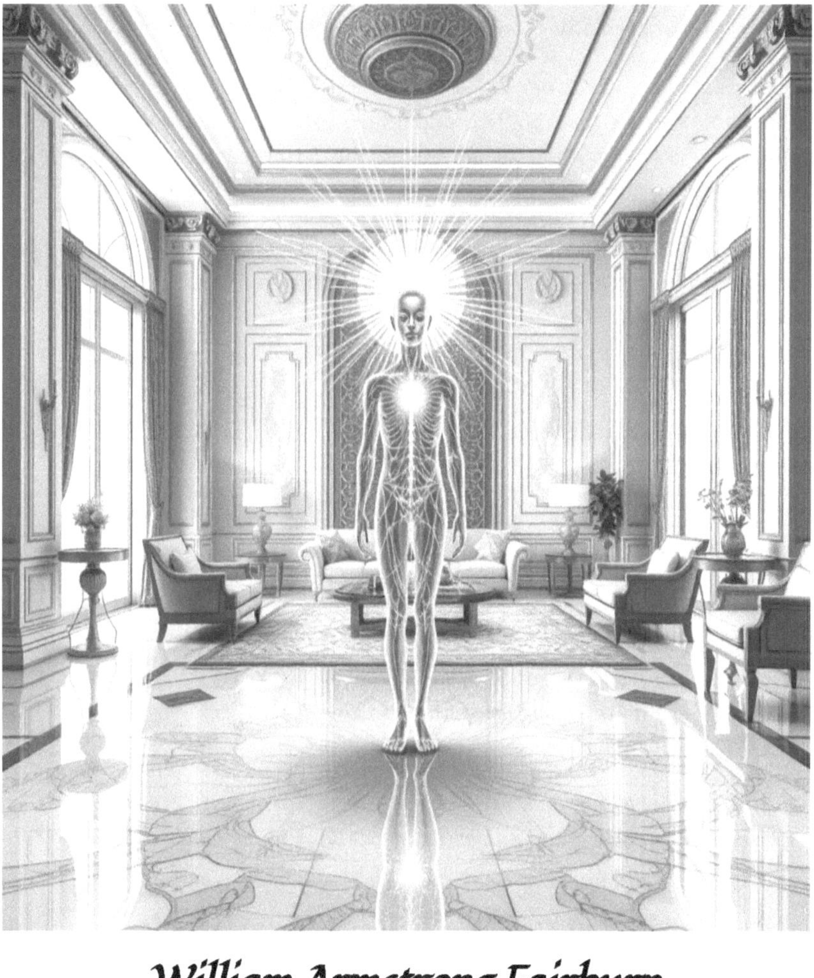

William Armstrong Fairburn

Publication Year: 2026
Publisher: DD Books
ISBN: 9789372449525

Edition: First Edition, 2026
Contact: ddsalesglobal@gmail.com

Book: Mentality and Freedom
Author: William Armstrong Fairburn
Price: Rs 350/-

Table of Content

Reader's Note

"Mentality and Freedom" by William Armstrong Fairburn is not just a book—it is a profound psychological expedition into the architecture of the human mind and the enduring struggle for freedom that defines our existence. It speaks to every individual who has ever questioned the balance between discipline and desire, between the power of will and the yearning for liberty. In a world that often confuses freedom with indulgence and willpower with rigidity, Fairburn offers a rare synthesis—an exploration of the mind as both the architect and the prisoner of its own destiny.

From the opening chapter, "The Power of a Disciplined Mind," Fairburn draws readers into the majestic tension between self-control and personal expression. The author does not preach asceticism but teaches mastery—the kind of mental clarity that liberates rather than restricts. This theme continues in "Mentality and Freedom," where he delves into the paradox of thought: how the intellect, when untamed, enslaves, and when guided, sets the soul free. The reader is invited to reflect on how true freedom begins not in external rebellion but in internal order.

In "Building Success Through Will and Action" and "Great Minds and Strong Wills," Fairburn elevates the discussion from reflection to practice. These chapters breathe with vitality—illustrating how the great figures of history achieved success not by chance but by a deliberate shaping of thought and habit. Each page inspires readers to see discipline as a form of liberation—a creative energy that transforms limitations into stepping stones.

The middle chapters, such as "Mental Discipline and the Moral Self" and "The Eternal Quest for Freedom," reach philosophical depth. They confront the reader with timeless questions: What does it mean to be free in a moral universe? Can a mind bound by impulse ever serve humanity? These sections resonate with both intellectual rigor and emotional force, challenging readers to look beyond material notions of success and seek inner sovereignty.

Later, in "The Cost of Passionate Will" and "The Quiet Call of Opportunity," the tone softens yet grows more profound. Fairburn's writing shifts from theory to the emotional human experience—the struggles, temptations, and quiet moments that test one's inner discipline. It is here that the book transcends philosophy and becomes wisdom literature—an exploration of the soul's education through effort, loss, and moral courage.

The concluding chapters—"Effort, Will, and Opportunity," "Life as a Struggle for Self and Service," and "The Art of Living and Working in the Machine Age"—bring the work into the modern era. Fairburn shows how the industrial and technological world challenges individuality, urging readers to retain humanity amidst machinery, to think freely amidst conformity, and to act with moral clarity in an age of noise and haste.

Finally, "The Power of Mental Flexibility and Broad Interests" concludes the journey by reminding readers that the highest form of discipline is adaptability—the open mind that can learn, unlearn, and grow continuously.

The beauty of "Mentality and Freedom" lies in its dual appeal: it is both intellectually enriching and spiritually nourishing. It connects deeply with modern readers who seek purpose amid distraction, ambition amid uncertainty, and morality amid material success. Fairburn's timeless insight offers more than instruction—it offers awakening. Each chapter feels like a dialogue between reason and spirit, giving readers not only ideas but an entire framework for living freely through disciplined thought.

To read "Mentality and Freedom" is to rediscover the art of thinking with precision, acting with courage, and living with moral strength. It is a guide for those who wish to lead—not just in career or ambition, but in life itself.

Publisher's Note

When *William Armstrong Fairburn* first penned *"Mentality and Freedom,"* he sought to examine the very roots of human capacity—the meeting point between self-mastery and self-expression. His aim was not to lecture, but to awaken a generation to the understanding that true freedom cannot exist without mental discipline, and that progress—whether personal or societal—depends upon the cultivation of a sound and purposeful mind.

This modern edition strives to bring Fairburn's powerful insights into clearer focus for today's readers. While the original text carries the elegance and intellectual depth of early twentieth-century thought, its message remains startlingly modern. The publisher's intent in this edition is not to alter Fairburn's meaning but to illuminate it—to offer accessibility without dilution, and clarity without compromise.

In an era where attention is fragmented and thought is often outsourced to machines, Fairburn's reflections on mental integrity and disciplined will feel more relevant than ever. The chapters on *The Power of a Disciplined Mind* and *Building Success Through Will and Action* echo with renewed urgency, reminding readers that the battle for freedom begins not in the outer world but within the boundaries of consciousness. Similarly, his examinations of *The Moral Self, Opportunity,* and *Effort* serve as quiet counsels for the modern age—urging balance between ambition and service, intellect and empathy.

As publishers, our goal is to ensure that Fairburn's timeless work reaches contemporary minds in its full clarity and dignity. The prose has been gently refined for flow and readability, yet every philosophical tone and intellectual weight of the author's voice remains intact. The structure and themes—ranging from willpower and character to moral freedom and mental flexibility—have been preserved as Fairburn intended: a complete and evolving journey of the human spirit toward freedom through mastery.

Readers today, living amidst speed, noise, and endless digital distractions, will find in these pages not only wisdom but also calm direction. The book offers a rare combination of intellectual engagement and emotional introspection. It speaks to leaders, thinkers, educators, and anyone who believes that life's highest art is to rule the self in order to serve the world.

This edition, therefore, honors *William Armstrong Fairburn* not only as a thinker but as a guide to the enduring challenge of modern humanity—the pursuit of freedom through disciplined thought. By preserving his original brilliance and making it accessible to the modern reader, we invite a new generation to explore the depths of their own mentality, and in doing so, to rediscover the meaning of true freedom.

Introduction

At its heart, *"Mentality and Freedom"* is an inquiry into one of life's greatest paradoxes: how can the human being be both bound by discipline and yet free in spirit? William Armstrong Fairburn, through his lucid and compelling chapters, invites readers to confront this question not as an abstract puzzle but as a living reality. His work explores how the disciplined mind—far from limiting freedom—becomes its truest instrument.

The book unfolds as a philosophical and psychological journey across thirteen chapters that together form a map of human self-mastery. It begins with *"The Power of a Disciplined Mind,"* where Fairburn establishes the foundation of his thesis: that mental discipline is not repression, but alignment—an act of harmonizing thought, emotion, and will. Through this harmony, man becomes free from confusion, fear, and external domination.

As the narrative deepens in *"Mentality and Freedom"* and *"Building Success Through Will and Action,"* Fairburn blends moral philosophy with practical insight. He portrays success not as a product of circumstance but as a triumph of inner order. His language is clear yet forceful, guiding readers to realize that freedom, in its highest form, is a victory over chaos—both internal and external. In subsequent chapters, the author introduces a moral dimension. Through *"Mental Discipline and the Moral Self"* and *"The Eternal Quest for Freedom,"* he transforms psychology into philosophy. Fairburn sees morality not as a restriction but as the spiritual geometry of freedom—the structure that gives liberty meaning. Freedom without moral foundation, he warns, becomes mere license; discipline without purpose becomes tyranny. True liberation, therefore, lies in the balanced development of will, intellect, and conscience.

By the time readers reach *"The Cost of Passionate Will"* and *"The Quiet Call of Opportunity,"* the work achieves emotional resonance. Fairburn shifts from intellectual reflection to human empathy. He speaks to the everyday struggles—ambition tempered by failure, effort followed by uncertainty—and shows how the disciplined mind turns adversity into opportunity. His tone is both encouraging and profoundly humane.

The later chapters expand the discussion to society and work. *"Life as a Struggle for Self and Service"* and *"The Art of Living and Working in the Machine Age"* reveal Fairburn's prophetic vision. He anticipates the dilemmas of modernity: the rise of mechanical labor, the erosion of individuality, and the spiritual fatigue of industrial civilization. Yet he offers hope—a blueprint for balancing progress with principle, efficiency with empathy, and productivity with purpose.

The closing chapter, *"The Power of Mental Flexibility and Broad Interests,"* serves as both culmination and revelation. It redefines discipline not as rigidity but as adaptability—the capacity to think broadly, feel deeply, and change wisely. Fairburn closes his work with the quiet wisdom that true freedom lies not in escape from structure, but in mastery of it.

To modern readers, *"Mentality and Freedom"* remains both intellectually challenging and deeply reassuring. It offers a pathway for anyone seeking to rise above confusion and mediocrity—to cultivate a mind that is both strong and supple, principled yet free. It appeals not only to philosophers and psychologists but to anyone seeking the higher art of living wisely in a restless age.

Fairburn's work is thus more than a study of mentality—it is a celebration of human potential. It invites readers to embark on a journey toward a kind of freedom that no circumstance can diminish: the freedom of a disciplined, awakened mind.

Chapter–1

The Power of a Disciplined Mind

Most people carry extraordinary abilities within them, yet live as if those abilities do not exist. Hidden talents, unused thoughts, and neglected mental strength quietly limit happiness, growth, and purpose. This chapter reveals why the mind weakens when left idle and grows powerful when actively used. It invites you to awaken dormant potential, exercise your thinking power, and transform unused inner riches into a living force that shapes a fuller, more meaningful life.

Most people have deep abilities and talents that they never discover or use. Even many of those we call "successful" don't come close to reaching their full potential. Their minds are like treasure chests filled with riches, but they only use a small part—sometimes without much care or purpose. Many people have several talents but only use one, and often that poorly. Instead of sharing their gifts with the world, they keep them hidden, unused.

As the poet said, "He who made us with such great abilities did not mean for them to lie unused." The greatest waste in the world is not money or resources—it is the waste of human minds. This waste slows progress and blocks happiness.

Bacon once said that if a person is only like an animal in body, but not connected to the great spirit through mind and soul, then he is missing what makes him truly human. Our mind is like a harp, sending the soul's message to the world. But how many of its strings are tuned and played? How many lie silent?

People naturally show the intelligence of animals, but much of the brain's unique power remains unused, weakened by mental laziness. We often use only a few familiar thoughts needed to get by in life, while large parts of our mind lie like unused land, unplanted and unproductive. Just like muscles, the mind must be exercised to stay strong. Thinking and feeling are like workouts for the brain—they increase blood flow and energy.

Nature's law is clear: use grows power, and lack of use causes decay. The more you practice something, the stronger it becomes; neglect leads to weakness. Talents that are used grow into greater skills and interests, while ignored talents fade away, turning great potential into ordinary life.

Life is thinking. The mind is what truly makes the body alive. Thoughts are the most powerful force we have. When they align with truth and purpose, they connect with the great forces that shape the world. Mental strength comes from using the mind actively—not from resting it. Idleness leads to emptiness. "A tree with no sap produces no fruit."

Imagine a ruined city—desolate and broken. Now imagine a city full of empty, abandoned buildings, waiting to be alive again. This empty city is like a mind that is neglected and unused—a place of ghostly silence and decay.

The mind needs not only to work but to be trained and exercised in the right way to keep its strength. As Locke said, ideas fade unless they are refreshed by thought and experience. Great qualities don't come from small efforts—they come from steady, focused practice and a clear purpose. A strong, healthy mind is the result of intelligent training and constant exercise.

Life is moving at a dizzying speed today; we live in a time full of extreme nervous tension. People face enormous pressure, and the pace of life is overwhelming. This rapid movement pushes us toward unnatural, shallow, and materialistic ways. People spin around like they're dizzy, rushing blindly in their daily routines. Their true selves become numb and lifeless. They lose balance, and their view of life and reality becomes unclear and unfocused. This fast, chaotic existence doesn't lead to meaningful energy or passion but rather a hollow emptiness—like a puppet's mind, abused and neglected, jerked around in a wild effort just to be part of life's show.

Simply breathing, walking, eating, and sleeping doesn't mean we are truly living. Even if all our body functions well, that doesn't guarantee strong health. Cicero wisely said, "The diseases of the mind are more destructive than those of the body." Even wrong ideas are better than no ideas at all because while error can trap us, inactivity and neglect destroy us. There is always hope for those trapped by wrong thoughts, but no hope for those who are mentally dead.

Today's world worships outward appearances. People are judged not by who they really are but by how they look. Society ranks people by money and fame, not by the quality of their mind or soul. When mental qualities are considered, they are judged by popular opinion—which always lags far behind true genius and forward thinkers. Two thousand years ago, Seneca taught a timeless lesson: "If you live according to nature, you will never be poor; if you live by the world's changing whims, you will never be rich."

Montaigne, in one of his essays, said, "It's strange that we only admire things for their outside qualities. We praise a horse for its strength and speed, not for its decorations. A greyhound is admired for its swiftness, not its collar. So why don't we value a man for what he truly is? People admire his followers, his grand house, his wealth, and his status, but these are just extras, not the man himself. If you buy a horse, you see it without saddle or clothes. So why judge a man only by his outer coverings? When judging a sword, we care about the quality of the blade, not the scabbard. A man should be judged by what he is inside. Take away his riches and honors and see him as he really is. Does he have a healthy body? What kind of mind does he have? Is it fair, capable, pure, calm, content, and brave in all situations?"

Epictetus once said that cattle care only for their food, and some men are just like cattle in their small-minded, materialistic thinking. He called all external things mere "fodder," saying, "To those busy with possessions, farms, servants, and public jobs, these things are nothing more than fodder." The real question to decide if a person's life is a success is not "What did he own?" but "What did he think and do?" or, simply, "What kind of mind did he have and how did he use it?"

"No matter how tall I am or how much of the ocean I can measure, I am measured by my soul: The mind is the true measure of a person."

The greatest goal for anyone is to make the most of their potential—to nurture every seed planted in their mind by the creative power of the universe. We must not neglect or waste any of our talents. Everyone is responsible for developing and using all the strengths they were born with. No one can say whose abilities will grow the most. Doing your best means using all your abilities with care and full effort. Saying "He did the best he could" often sounds like an excuse for failure. True strength is giving everything you have—no half-effort, no drifting with the crowd, but working with strong purpose, energy, passion, and results. The person who does all they can within their circumstances "does well and acts nobly; even angels could do no more."

In today's artificial world, people often ignore their amazing gifts. They follow the crowd without thinking and copy the popular opinions without question. In the 20th century, the hardest challenge is to truly think—to use your mind honestly and individually, with reason and logic. Many gifted people—philosophers, scientists, artists—fail to use their talents fully and only carry symbols of their failure.

We live in a time where people are never satisfied with their wealth or their minds. As Deshouliere said, "No one is satisfied with their fortune, nor dissatisfied with their intellect." It would be wonderful if everyone could have a sudden awakening like Saul of Tarsus, seeing clearly the real values and the outcomes of all life's paths. The more shallow a person is, the more self-satisfied they appear. Remember the wise warning of Quarles:"Always be unhappy with who you are if you want to become who you are not; for when you are pleased with yourself, there you will remain." Self-satisfaction is the most useless state; instead of bragging about what we have done, we should spend time finding and fixing our faults—no easy task, even for the best.

We often hear this is the age of specialists, but that is no reason for a person with many talents to use only one. A narrow specialist might add to knowledge, but a person who develops their mind in many areas is a stronger specialist. They see not only their narrow field but also the larger picture and related forces. A person with one great talent becomes even greater by developing all their lesser talents. This well-rounded growth turns a mere fanatic into a true genius and a leader.

"Every idea," Emerson said, "that genius and devotion bring into the world changes it," and Carlyle added, "In every age, the greatest event is the arrival of a Thinker." But most people drift into jobs that only demand a narrow set of skills. They earn a living, do what's expected, settle into a routine, and begin to operate almost like machines, using their subconscious mind without much thought. When faced with new or difficult situations, their minds grow dull and less sharp. Soon, they fall into a mental sleep and, as a force in the world, they die early – without really contributing to progress or success.

Epictetus compares such a person to a traveler who, on his way home, stops at a nice inn and decides to stay there forever. The traveler forgets his original goal. When asked, "Weren't you traveling through this place?" he replies, "But this inn is so comfortable." Yet there are many other good inns and beautiful places ahead, meant only as stops on the journey. Many people stop just like that traveler, settling too soon and wasting their lives as if trapped by temptation.

This waste of purpose, motivation, and direction is what makes life dull, boring, and unexciting. This way of thinking leads to monotony and sadness, covering the soul with a heavy blanket of despair. A person may gain wealth and power and be called successful, but if they act like machines focused only on money or control, neglecting their mind and higher qualities, their life is incomplete. Can we truly compare the mental and spiritual life of a person to their purely physical and material existence?

"It is better to fail aiming high than to succeed in a low aim."

Think of the human brain as a house with many rooms. Some people live in just one or two rooms, rarely exploring the others—rooms filled with great ideas and feelings. Many fill their minds with only worldly things that have a price, forgetting the rooms meant for love, joy, beauty, and worship. Beecher described such people as having apartments in their souls once filled with taste and love, now abandoned and replaced with material things. He also said many build their lives like cathedrals: the parts near the ground look finished, but the towers and spires that reach for the sky remain unfinished forever. Fuller expressed this too, saying that often the attic—the highest part—is empty in those who seem tall and grand.

The brain can be seen as a three-story house with a basement. As humans evolved, they added floors to this house. The basement, called the cerebellum, is primitive and connected to basic, animal-like instincts. The first floor handles senses, survival, aggression, and basic desires—what we can call the "animal" part. The second floor developed as humans began to think and reason more deeply; it is the "human" or "material" level, where critical and thoughtful powers live. The top floor is the "ethical" level, designed to hold the qualities that make us truly human—morality, ethics, respect, ideals, kindness, honesty, justice, and consistency.

Many people, gifted with this three-story brain, refuse to spend time upstairs. They seldom visit the highest floor where true success lives.

Each floor of the brain-house is divided into rooms, with front rooms and back rooms. Scientists say that the room of Domesticity—like the kitchen in a home—is at the back, while the important intellectual rooms are at the front. As humans evolved from animals, the front part of the brain, along with the top, grew stronger.

Some people live like in old-fashioned houses with only a kitchen and a simple living room, called "But" and "Ben" by the Scots. They keep the front, best room closed most of the time, only opening it for Sundays or special occasions. In the same way, many people rarely use the front part of their brain—the intellectual part—and their amazing mental abilities stay unused and inactive.

Epictetus said humans are rational beings, set apart from wild and domesticated animals by their ability to think and reason. He warned, "Be careful not to act like wild beasts, or you lose your humanity. Acting greedily, lustfully, or without thought lowers us to the level of cattle, destroying our rational mind. Acting angrily, violently, or passionately makes us like wild animals. Some are like wolves—crafty and untrustworthy; others like lions—wild and fierce; but most are like foxes—dishonest and sneaky even among animals. A man who spreads lies and ill will is worse than a fox."

The brain is like a library, divided into sections on different subjects, each with shelves full of books. How many people spend their whole life reading only one shelf or section? This limits them and stops them from living a full, well-rounded life. Reading is the best way to gain knowledge, expand your view, and spark new ideas. Books cover every field of knowledge and effort. A good library holds all this wisdom. Carlyle said, "Everything mankind has done or thought is safely kept in the pages of books. Today's true university is a library."

A well-rounded mind is like a library with shelves full of books that are used often, not dusty and forgotten. But most people refuse not only to think deeply but also to read the right books—those that make them think, awaken hidden talents, and push them to act. "A good book is one that makes me want to work." Reading newspapers, light novels, or "time-killer" material is not real reading. It's fine to spend a little time each day on news, but as a society, we waste time on shallow magazines and bestsellers that are to literature what ragtime music is to serious music.

Reading books that challenge and inspire takes effort, focus, and practice. Yet, very few people, even those who could understand serious ideas, are willing to train their minds to absorb and benefit from true literature.

We wouldn't start teaching a child calculus before they learn basic math. We begin with simple addition and subtraction, then move to multiplication and division, and after years of steady effort, the child can handle complex problems. The same careful approach is needed in reading and choosing books, though all reading can teach us something valuable.

Epictetus wisely said, "Some people try to swallow whole books they cannot digest. They throw them up or get sick. Such people need to know their limits. Nothing great is created suddenly—no bunch of grapes or figs appears in an hour. First, the tree must blossom, then bear fruit, then ripen. So don't expect to instantly master the fruit of the mind."

Books are treasure houses of knowledge and wisdom. They keep the thoughts, discoveries, and insights of the past. When filled with truth, books live forever, defying time. The classics of ancient times are fountains of learning and deep wisdom. They spread eternal truths and freedom in a world easily led into error and bondage. They inspire thought, strengthen willpower, and encourage reason and logic—just as they did thousands of years ago.

An ancient wise man said that even in his time, the world needed people who would live by the eternal truths found in books—people whose actions would prove their belief in those truths.

Reading and studying are to the mind what exercise is to the body. The quality, type, and amount of mental exercise are all important for success. Just like the body grows stronger through careful training, the mind stays healthy, sharp, and powerful when we use it wisely. Epictetus asked, "Do you want to see the strength of a philosopher? It is a will that doesn't give up, avoids harm, uses its powers fully, makes careful decisions, and follows steady resolve."

Philosophy begins with a desire to learn and grow mentally, along with the awareness of our own weaknesses and unused talents. The true goal of education is to fully develop all the abilities we have. The more we learn, the more we realize how much we don't know. But education leads to a broad, deep enjoyment of life—one that comes from using our abilities to serve a greater purpose.

Plato said, "It is better never to be born than to live without learning, because ignorance brings trouble." It's surprising how ignorance often lives side-by-side with pride, showing itself as vanity, arrogance, and selfishness. Ignorance is darkness, forgetting, and mental death. It is the root cause of war, hatred, disease, poverty, and cruelty. Ignorance is the opposite of truth; it feeds on selfishness, wears the clothes of ego, worships superstition, and leaves pain and death behind.

Epictetus taught that every habit grows stronger by practice. If you want to be a reader, read. If you want to be a writer, write. After sitting still for many days, try to walk far and you will see how weak your legs have become. The same happens with the mind. Whatever skill you want to improve, practice it regularly.

Many people try to avoid mental effort. They ignore the challenges that would develop their natural mental powers. Some proudly claim to be strong-minded, but their reasoning is weak and frozen. "We all fear physical paralysis and try hard to avoid it; yet no one worries about a mental paralysis." People with one idea are often lost in a single obsession—too much in one direction and too little in others. But even these are better than the majority, who have no personal ideas or original thoughts and cannot think for themselves.

The biggest challenge for a person is to control outside influences and free the true inner self. Success comes from breaking free of materialism and empty social rules that lack reason and purpose. We must strengthen our will so it works naturally—noble, free, faithful, humble, and unhindered. Such a life becomes a powerful, positive force in the world, leaving no room for regret, despair, or false idols.

As Goethe said, "What dazzles only shines for a moment; what is real lasts forever."

Right now, the world needs thinkers—people who use reason, are honest with themselves, analyze deeply, and study with clear goals.

A truly successful person develops all parts of the brain, no matter what their role in life. Such a person is kind, understanding, and able to think carefully. A leader who uses only part of their brain, leaving other parts weak, cannot be fair or caring. They cannot understand others fully, and this limits their judgment. The same is true for workers at every level.

People who have nothing to offer often see little worth in others. Narrow vision and selfishness, caused by a lack of mental growth, are behind many workplace conflicts. Both bosses and workers often share the blame. Remember Voltaire's words: those who are unfair become harsh, and those who lack wisdom become sad.

The only way to real peace and efficiency in work is through education that teaches thoughtful learning.

Confucius said, "Learning without thought is useless; thought without learning is dangerous."

Politics and selfish ignorance will keep causing problems between employers and employees until most people learn to see things clearly and fairly. Eventually, governments will serve the people justly, protecting every individual and group—not ignoring or abusing them as often happens now.

It takes time for the world to learn that harm to one hurts all. Unfair wages, unreasonable profits, broken systems, too much power in few hands, and special privileges all damage the state and its people.

Many people complain that they cannot move forward or find better opportunities. But often, these are the same people who have never truly tried to improve themselves or prepare for greater responsibilities. A worker who never reads, studies, or thinks will stay at his workbench forever. A foreman who day after day only watches others do the same tasks without learning how to improve the work or make it more efficient will not keep his position forever. Eventually, he will lose his place—becoming a victim of progress and the rule that only the fittest survive.

A manager who stops trying, becomes lazy, and loses interest in learning or leading progress will soon be replaced by someone who uses their mind fully. That thinker and hard worker climbs higher because he is never satisfied with where he stands. He always sees new possibilities ahead, pushing him forward to explore and succeed even more.

No matter how dedicated someone is to their job, if they do not put their full mind into it and spend their free time improving themselves, they will not be valuable to their organization.

Education is the great force that lifts the world up. Growing mentally breaks down barriers between social classes. Many poor boys carry within them the seeds of great minds and can become future leaders if they develop their talents. A man's physical ability to work may be worth a few dollars a day, but his true value lies in his mind—and this value depends on how much he chooses to develop his mind.

Many men with only one or two talents but a well-trained brain will surpass others who have many talents but do not realize or develop them. We hear that humans are only about 50% physically efficient due to health limits, but if we could see clearly how much of our mental potential we actually use, the difference would be shocking.

It is time to stop thinking that education ends when we leave school. It barely begins there. School teaches us how to learn, but true education continues all through life. The world may ignore or reject a person at first, but it eventually respects the person who keeps growing in mind and spirit—who fights against the current, uses time wisely, and achieves something worthy, no matter how small. Such a person helps move the world closer to its highest goals.

As Longfellow said, "Not in the shouts and plaudits of the throng, But in ourselves are triumphs and defeat."

Chapter–2

Mentality and Freedom

Is intelligence really decided by the size of the brain, or by how it is used? This chapter explores the difference between raw brain capacity and active mental development. It shows why balance, use, and training of the mind matter more than size alone, and how every person—regardless of background—can grow intelligence through thoughtful effort, education, and healthy mental exercise.

In all living creatures, the size and development of a body part usually show how strong or active it is. When we compare similar materials under similar conditions, size often means power. For example, you wouldn't compare pine wood to cast iron, or cast iron to steel without considering their different strengths. In engineering, even when choosing steel, we look at its strength, flexibility, and other qualities before deciding if it will do the job.

Just like we expect a blacksmith to have strong arms or a wrestler to have broad shoulders, we often think that a larger brain means greater intelligence. When we look at the brains of different animals, their mental ability tends to match the size of their brains compared to their bodies. Anthropologists say a fox and a groundhog have nearly the same body size, but the fox's brain is four times heavier. A crow has a much bigger brain than a turkey, and the crow is known for being much smarter. An eagle, with half the body size of a goose, has twice the brain capacity.

Humans have brains that look like those of great apes, but ours are three to four times larger. Compared to body weight, humans have about five times the brain size of their closest animal relatives. For example, a horse weighs nine times more than a man but has only a quarter of his brain volume. Elephants and whales have larger brains than humans but are less intelligent because their brain size compared to body size is much smaller. In humans, the ratio is about 1 to 37, in elephants 1 to 500, and in whales 1 to 3000.

In animals, intelligence mainly depends on brain size. Larger-brained, smarter animals have replaced less intelligent ones over time.

The huge reptiles of the past were replaced by mammals, and now humans, with the largest brains, stand at the top of animal life. Fossil studies show that human brain size has increased over time, starting from early humans with brains like those of the highest apes.

But in humans, brain size alone doesn't measure intelligence. It matters how much of the brain's power is used and how well it is organized. A smaller brain that is well structured and used can be smarter than a larger brain that is inactive or poorly organized. Some famous thinkers had very large brains, but so did some ordinary people. For example, a man named Rustan, who was uneducated, reportedly had one of the largest brains ever recorded. He might have been a great thinker if he had developed his abilities, even if his body was not impressive. What counts most is not how big the brain is, but how much a person uses it.

All healthy people have enough brain power to contribute to the world's progress if they develop and use their minds. Even the most "ignorant" groups have brain sizes close to other races. When children from these groups get good education and a stimulating environment, they often match or even surpass the achievements of children from more privileged backgrounds. This shows that brain quality can be improved by environment and education, not just heredity.

Every person is born with certain brain abilities, tendencies, and qualities. How much they use their natural talents, develop different brain areas, and train their mental powers determines their success in life as intelligent beings.

People from cold northern climates, like the blond Caucasians known for being strong and conquering, tend to have larger brains.

This is because survival in harsh conditions requires using the mind to find food, build homes, protect oneself, and fight smartly. In contrast, life in the tropics has placed fewer demands on the mind, leading to different development.

Some argue that brain size doesn't show intelligence because some mentally ill people have large brains. Mental illness can result from overstressing parts of the brain or ignoring mental health.

For example, a great mathematician lost his mind by focusing too hard without rest. Another who memorized too many facts became mentally exhausted because he neglected other mental skills.

Genius often comes with a touch of madness, and people sometimes call this "eccentricity of genius" when one mental ability is highly developed but others suffer. For true success, the brain must be well balanced and developed evenly, as much as life and practical needs allow. Mental illness can happen when one part of the brain is overstressed, like a string pulled too tight. People with larger brains today are more likely to have one skill overdeveloped because of modern specialization, compared to those with smaller brains.

Some people, called microcephalic idiots, have extremely small brains—sometimes weighing as little as 8 to 10 ounces. Scientists say normal intelligence is unlikely if the brain weighs less than about 32 ounces. The average healthy adult brain weighs between 48 and 50 ounces. Experts agree that brain size generally shows mental ability, especially when the brain is healthy and actively used. The sharper and better organized the brain's structure, the higher the quality of thought.

When comparing brains, it's best to focus on the cerebrum—the main thinking part of the brain. However, most measurements include the entire brain mass inside the skull, which also covers parts with different jobs. This method isn't accurate for judging intelligence, since it treats all brain matter as equal, no matter its role or quality.

Think of the brain like a warehouse. Some warehouses are full of valuable goods, while others hold lower-quality or unused materials. Sometimes goods decay or lose value if they are left unused too long. Owners lose money when valuable goods sit idle instead of being used to meet demand.

So, what about our mental warehouse? Life demands it be filled—but with what? Are we filling our brains with useful, valuable knowledge? Are we using and renewing what we learn, or are our mental stores gathering dust? Imagine if a skilled assessor evaluated the true worth of your mental "warehouse" and its contents.

The brain mostly contains two types of material: (1) gray matter, made up of cells and key to mental activity, and (2) white matter, made of firm, tubular fibers. The gray matter forms folds called cerebral convolutions on the brain's surface. Scientists agree that the larger and more complex these folds, the greater the brain's mental power—assuming the brain's quality remains constant.

Intelligent people have many complex folds in their gray matter. These folds become simpler as we look at animals with less intelligence, disappearing entirely in the lowest forms of life. People with weak minds or intellectual disabilities have simple brain folds and less gray matter. On the other hand, famous scholars and world leaders have brains with very complex gray matter folds.

Huxley once said that the brains of chimpanzees and orangutans differ only slightly from humans in small ways. Those small differences are mainly in the complexity of the gray matter folds. Apes have simple brain folds, similar to a human with low intelligence.

Another expert, Turner, pointed out that the sensory and motor parts of the brain in children, monkeys, and even primitive humans look very similar. What really makes the difference is the complexity of the brain areas responsible for thought and reasoning.

So, it's not just the total brain weight that matters but how much gray matter—the thinking part—is present. Since the thickness of this layer is about the same in all brains, the complexity of its folds shows how much mental power it has. Brain cells are found mainly in these folds, which relates to our conscious thoughts and feelings.

The brain is where thought, feeling, and awareness come from. It gathers all the signals from our body and sends out commands to control movement and action. It also works with other nervous system parts that manage important life functions like breathing, digestion, and circulation, keeping us alive and well.

It was truly wise that human will does not have full control over every part of the brain and nervous system. Our physical health and even life itself depend on certain automatic functions beyond conscious control. If we could control every part of our brain and body all the time—even during sleep—life would be very short, and we would never reach full maturity. Imagine if a person in their prime tried to control every nerve and muscle consciously, treating all parts like they do the ones they can control easily. That person would quickly wear out and likely fail.

The gray matter in our brain is where the mind lives. Different parts of this gray matter handle different mental abilities, and how well these parts work depends on their size, activity, and the brain's overall quality. The brain was made to be used regularly and actively. It receives a rich supply of blood compared to other body parts because it needs constant nourishment. The brain is also a highly organized machine made of specialized parts.

Modern science has proven what many had guessed: each part of the brain handles a specific mental task—this is called cerebral localization. For example, W. Hanna Thomson showed that if one area of gray matter is damaged, a person can lose their sight even though their eyes and nerves are fine. Similarly, damage to another part can cause loss of hearing, even if the ears are perfectly healthy. This means that sight and hearing don't happen in the eyes or ears themselves; those are just tools connected to certain brain areas. The brain's gray matter is crucial—any damage or disturbance to it can affect all mental processes. Injuries to the brain often cause strange mental problems, sometimes even changing a person's personality or moral character. To show how specific brain areas control different skills, Professor Hinshelwood of Glasgow told of a well-educated man who suddenly became "word-blind" for English—he couldn't read English anymore. But since he knew Greek, Latin, and French, tests found he could read Greek perfectly, Latin fairly well, and French with difficulty. The injury affected the English word recognition area most, the French area a bit, and barely touched the Latin and Greek areas.

Hinshelwood also described a Frenchman in Glasgow who, after a stroke, became unable to hear French words, but still understood English perfectly. After his brain injury, people had to speak to him only in English.

Thomson shared the story of a patient who lost the ability to speak after an umbrella accidentally injured the part of his brain responsible for speech—yet no other abilities were lost. A tiny piece of gray matter, no bigger than a hazelnut, holds every word a person can say. If this part is destroyed, the person can understand words but cannot speak any.

Professor Edgren of Stockholm wrote about people who lost the ability to read music due to brain injury, while their word-reading skills remained. Some music lovers suffered from "amusic," losing the ability to recognize musical themes or tell great compositions from simple tunes. Many such cases show how damage to specific brain areas can cause loss of certain mental skills or changes in personality.

All mental processes happen in the brain's gray matter, a thin layer that covers the brain and is only about 1/12 to 1/8 of an inch thick. Some say that brain size or skull capacity alone doesn't fully measure intelligence. But when the brain grows larger, its surface area also grows—a lot. Just like when you increase the size of a cube, its volume grows faster than its surface area. The human brain isn't smooth; it has many folds and wrinkles. These folds increase the surface area of gray matter, which relates directly to mental power.

People's brains differ a lot in size, shape, and quality of nerve tissue. No two brains are exactly the same. Yet, every normal person has enough gray matter to develop strong mental abilities and succeed if they choose to. Thomson, in his book *Brain and Personality*, said that while people may be born with different natural talents, the real mental skills come from learning and experience, not just inheritance. He's right to an extent—brains develop and change as we learn. But some brains are naturally more organized and delicate, like silk compared to wool. You can fold silk to fit more in a small space, just like a better brain can hold more knowledge and ideas.

We are born with both natural brain powers and instincts. These can help or sometimes block our growth. Some instincts guide us toward talents, while others make it harder to learn new things or adjust to the modern world. Scientists say there are two types of brain functions—instinctive (inherited) and learned (developed through experience). For animals and humans who can learn, the less they depend on inherited instincts, the more their brains can grow by learning.

The size and shape of the brain are mostly inherited, though some changes can happen in early life. The quality and texture of brain tissue are also inherited, like skin texture or hair type. But the real power of the brain comes from the will—our personality and determination—that grows with us. It's this inner drive that makes a brain great or causes it to remain average. It's said, "A strong personality can make a great brain, but no brain alone can create a great personality."

The brain's power depends on both the amount of gray matter and how actively it is used. A beginner at the piano may only make a few random sounds, while an expert brings beautiful music from the same keys. In the same way, a person without the will to learn can only produce weak ideas, but a determined thinker, who keeps learning and focusing, can produce powerful thoughts that contribute to progress and success. We should use all parts of the brain, not just a few. Neglecting parts of the brain is like a conductor trying to lead a symphony without the strings or woodwinds—important parts are missing, and the music won't be complete. It's strange that people who use only a small part of their mental abilities would think it silly to use only one leg or arm, not realizing how important full use is.

It's often said that humans have two brains but use only one fully, so no matter how educated we are, we are only about 50% mentally efficient. Humans are built symmetrically, with paired organs like eyes, ears, lungs, and limbs. This natural dual design suggests great potential if both sides of the brain and body are fully used.

The main reason our organs come in pairs is probably to protect us during emergencies and also for ease and efficiency in daily use. But having two of an organ doesn't mean we get double the power or ability. For example, having two good ears doesn't make a person hear twice as well as someone with one ear. Similarly, losing one eye doesn't mean we see only half as well as someone with two eyes. Even if a person loses one kidney, the other kidney can grow stronger and handle the work of both.

It's proven that, except for hands and feet, either organ in a pair can do the job alone if needed. Both eyes see the same things, both ears hear the same sounds; one eye does not see only some colors while the other sees the rest. Likewise, one ear does not hear only low sounds while the other hears only high sounds. So, having paired organs is like having a backup plan. Nature wisely designed us this way, ensuring that if one part fails, the other can take over. This isn't because we need double the power all the time, but as a safety measure—like an army being only as strong as its reserves. The human brain is also divided into two halves—right and left—similar to other paired organs. But here, each half controls the opposite side of the body. The right half controls the left side, and the left half controls the right. If one side of the brain is damaged, the body side it controls becomes paralyzed. However, losing one half of the brain doesn't mean losing mental ability. The brain doesn't produce thoughts automatically like an organ producing juice. Instead, the brain is a tool used by the thinker, who can choose which half to use.

Experts say that people tend to use only one half of their brain for thinking, and which half they use depends on chance or habit formed in childhood. When we learn or store knowledge, it usually goes into one brain half only. If that half becomes damaged, relearning the same knowledge with the other half can take much longer.

From childhood, most people develop habits of using one hand more than the other—usually the right hand—because of teaching or natural preference.

This leads to one-sidedness: most people can't use their weaker hand well. This habit also shapes which brain half is more active. Because learning is easier when we're young, teaching both hands to be equally skilled (ambidexterity) from childhood could lead to more balanced brain development.

It is believed that right-handed people mostly use the left brain for speech and thinking, while left-handed people use the right brain. Early humans were probably naturally ambidextrous, and many young children show this ability before society teaches them to favor one hand.

Training children to be ambidextrous wouldn't cause any harm; in fact, it might help develop their brains more evenly. It wouldn't double their intelligence, since using two ears doesn't double hearing ability. But it might keep the brain healthier and more flexible, helping it learn and adapt better, especially if one half is injured later in life.

It is very unlikely that both halves of the brain can be fully trained at the same time. If that were possible, ambidexterity would be such a huge advantage that every thoughtful person would want to develop it. Still, in an ambidextrous person, some knowledge might be stored in one half of the brain, and other knowledge in the other half. Because there would be no natural preference for one side, if one brain half got damaged, only part of the knowledge would be lost—not everything learned over many years.

This idea about brain halves and paired organs doesn't change the fact that brain size doesn't determine intelligence. What matters is how much and how well a person uses their brain.

The size, weight, or surface of the brain only show a person's natural potential, not how well they are using it. You can't easily know which half of your brain you are actually using because the brain is symmetrical in shape.

But what is important is that often one half of the brain is fully developed and used, while the other half remains less active, even though both halves take up the same space.

The brain is a flexible, adaptable organ that can be shaped and trained. This training changes the physical structure of the brain. However, this flexibility decreases with age, especially when learning new languages or complex mental skills.

What we learn easily can also be easily forgotten. The brain's ability to bounce back to its original state shows its plasticity.

Think of the brain like a soft, moldable surface where the will imprints what it wants to learn, much like how a record is made on a talking machine. Sometimes it takes repeated practice for the brain to record an idea clearly so we can recall it perfectly later. Other times, one powerful experience or thought leaves such a strong mark that it lasts a lifetime.

How clear and lasting a memory or idea is depends on many things: how focused we are, how interested or involved we feel, how important the idea seems, and even how strongly it affects us emotionally. The will not only controls how impressions are received and recorded but also how and when we recall them. Like a needle running through the grooves of a record, the brain can bring back a memory, a word, a tune, or a picture just as it was first experienced.

To be truly educated, the human mind must be trained and practiced. Knowledge comes from learning, and learning requires effort. Success follows when attention meets hard work. Attention means having a strong desire to learn, thinking deeply, and focusing fully. Work means using your energy wisely and applying yourself with purpose. Being active is living; being lazy is like being dead inside.

Discipline is not about stopping activity—it's about guiding and controlling it.

A disciplined mind focuses its energy in the right direction. It doesn't just skim over the surface like a butterfly on flowers but digs deep for truth and facts. It keeps going until success is reached.

When learning something new, the mind must be ready to go through a long, sometimes hard process, building knowledge step by step. As we grow older, we often want to skip the basics and jump to advanced ideas, but that doesn't work. There are no shortcuts to true knowledge. The path to learning, designed by the great Cosmic Mind, is always uphill and rough. Yet, for those who truly seek truth, this journey is both rewarding and exciting. The time spent learning is time well spent and full of joy.

For a true seeker, gaining knowledge expands the soul. The mind grows stronger and nourished by mental food, just as the body is fed by physical food. A thinker stays grounded in reality and connected to others, but also lifts their spirit beyond the limits of everyday life. As Huxley said, such a person "stands on a mountain top, transformed by the light of infinite truth."

At birth, each person is given a brain—a highly organized chamber of nerve matter full of potential. This brain is a gift, but how much it develops depends on how the person shapes it. Some brains may be naturally more flexible or sensitive, and some people may have more or less brain matter than others. But in the end, each person must build their own mental power.

We should not focus on the limits we inherit from birth because no one ever fully reaches their true potential anyway. Instead, we should ask ourselves what we are doing with the brain and mind we have. Imagine having one hundred areas of opportunity in the brain—how many are we really using? How well are we using them? If we could measure our total mental efficiency, what would it be?

Even the finest brain is useless if left inactive. Only a strong human will, working with the laws of nature, can bring this powerful instrument to life.

Through focused, steady effort, the mind can awaken and share its unique message with the world, becoming an important part of the great symphony of life.

Chapter-3

Building Success Through Will and Action

Life does not shape us—we shape ourselves. This chapter reveals how strong will, focused effort, and right thinking turn potential into real success. It shows why challenges are not enemies but builders of inner strength, and how discipline, persistence, and clear purpose separate those who merely wish from those who truly achieve.

A person shapes and builds their mind just like a craftsman shapes his work. Much of life is what we make of it; happiness comes as a reward for hard work done well, while unhappiness usually follows carelessness, wrong thinking, laziness, and ignoring the natural laws of life.

Life is movement, activity, and effort. We achieve whatever we truly want enough to work for. Challenges and obstacles are not just problems—they help build our mental strength, endurance, and willpower. A strong and determined will does not accept defeat; it always stands ready to face the challenges life throws in the quest for knowledge, truth, and what is right. As Sturgis Ingersoll said, "No one is so lucky as to win life's prizes without a fight, and no one is so unlucky as to lack the desire—even if hidden deep inside—to fight."

Success comes from focused effort and hard work. Many average people complain about bad luck, blame the lack of chances for their failure or mediocrity, and blame fate. But successful people create their own chances, jump over obstacles, break down barriers, laugh at the idea of luck, use their inner strength, and put their energy into achieving results—not making excuses. In one case, the will is weak, soft, and ineffective; in the other, it is strong like tempered steel—flexible but unbreakable, powerful, and determined.

Many people have great potential and strong minds but fail because they do not truly want success. They may think they do, but they don't really understand what willpower means. Success requires full, steady, and consistent commitment to a goal, along with smart choices and cutting away what is unnecessary. We pursue things that help us grow and improve, and avoid negative, harmful habits—even if they seem tempting.

Using the will properly means making continuous effort, sometimes giving up pleasures early in life for what might seem like a distant reward—the joy of serving a purpose. But as we grow, reality becomes clear, and real achievement brings deep satisfaction inside. The biggest battle in life is often with ourselves, not just with the world. The hardest fight is not against some "inborn sin," but against the soul-crushing laziness and lack of care for using our energy well or seeing our true potential for usefulness and success. The greatest gift would be a clear inner vision that forces us to see ourselves honestly—our faults, missed chances, and all the opportunities waiting to be reached.

Eliot said, "No one has the right to find life dull or unrewarding if they see anything they can fix or any weakness in themselves they can work to overcome." The problem for most people is they refuse to look inside themselves. Even if they try, their view is clouded by pride and self-satisfaction, so they don't truly see. Yet they are quick to judge others and see many faults in the world around them. When looking at their own faults, they use a magnifying glass, but when looking at others, they use a telescope, making their own mistakes seem small and others' mistakes huge. Confucius wisely said, "People neglect their own fields and rush to weed others' fields. They demand much from others but give little to themselves."

In business, people carefully count and check their stock; every raw material and product is measured and valued. In a well-run factory, the state of materials and work in progress is always known, and production machines are kept in top shape. Why don't we do the same with our minds? Why don't we take stock of our mental abilities, check how well our brain works, and evaluate the quality of our thoughts? A business owner knows if they have ten or five cases of something in their warehouse and knows the value of every item. But most people have no idea if their mind produces many or few good thoughts, or care about the quality or value of what they think.

Success begins when we manage our mind like a valuable business—knowing what we have, using it wisely, and always working to improve it.

In a well-run factory, every part works together—creation, effort, and power are active in all departments, each using energy efficiently to produce a valuable, complete product. It is useless to have one section running perfectly if other parts are falling behind or shut down because of lack of help, energy, materials, poor plans, or weak leadership.

A successful factory runs like a smooth cycle, with all parts coordinated and working as a team. Every machine, every department must produce its full share of quality work on time.

Imagine if a person's brain worked like such a well-organized factory, managed wisely and smoothly, with every part in harmony and led by a skilled and understanding leader. Think of the power and success that mind could have in the world.

A truly efficient person understands the art of living well and makes the best use of what nature has given. They pay attention to every part of their life and mind—nothing is ignored. This person is hardworking, careful, but also deeply human—strong, kind, approachable, and lovable. As Dresser said, "Efficiency is not just about work; it is about life as a whole. It is a human matter." An efficient person is flexible, thoughtful, and ready to act. Their brain is made for action, developed by doing, and their success depends on turning mental wisdom into real-world results.

True greatness comes from balanced development. A brain that grows too much in one area but neglects others is not truly great. Just like a person with a body that grows oddly in one part might become a circus act, an unbalanced mind is not healthy or useful. A person who only focuses on one talent, like making money, but ignores other parts of their mind, is incomplete. Even if their goal seems good, they are not fully efficient and may even cause harm by being out of balance.

If we saw someone writing brilliant books but refusing to exercise their body, we would say their work doesn't justify neglecting nature's laws. With good exercise and care, they could write even better. Refusing to use and develop any part of the brain is like refusing to use a hand, leg, or one of the senses. People quickly notice and dislike physical defects because they affect daily life, but why don't they notice mental weaknesses in the same way? Confucius said, "When a man's finger is deformed, he knows he should be unhappy, but if his mind is deformed, he does not know he should be unhappy. This is ignorance about what matters most."

Today, the world needs minds as beautifully formed as the perfect bodies of the ancient Greeks—strong, balanced, and graceful. The Greeks believed in exercise to develop the body, knowing that muscles and brain both grow with use. But their greatest honors didn't go to specialists in one sport, but to those who won the Pentathlon—a competition testing five different skills. This showed true all-around excellence.

The Greeks admired physical perfection and lived their ideals by practicing sports themselves. They were very different from Roman nobles who only watched. No one can develop body or mind by watching others; growth comes from personal effort.

When we look at mental qualities, it's hard to say which are the most important because all matter. Dr. Johnson said, "A truly strong mind is one that values both great and small things equally." Even small parts are essential—like tiny bolts in a machine that keep it running. Some qualities may seem minor or useless, but without them, true success and greatness cannot be reached.

Using every part of your brain fully and living every minute of every hour—that is success, and it brings true happiness. Real joy never comes without some effort. Action is what shows a person's true worth. Our will, which guides our mind, is what controls everything we do. It is the highest power in us.

The will is like a General commanding an army, in charge of every force nature has given. The General must train, organize, and lead these forces, making sure every part works efficiently together.

No wise General would go to battle with only a small force. They need infantry, cavalry, artillery, engineers, signal teams, transport, medical aid—all working in harmony under one strong leader. Similarly, to succeed, a person must manage all parts of their mind and body together, controlling and directing their efforts skillfully toward their goals. The human will is the central leader of the mind, just as discipline is crucial in the military for winning battles. Strong, focused control is shown by clear, balanced results—whether in armies or businesses. Without a strong leader, there is confusion and chaos. If the controlling power is weak, too much effort goes one way, too little another, or plans keep changing, leading to failure.

The "General" of the mind commands many different forces. Some parts may be untrained, like raw recruits, but it is his job to train them into strong, reliable fighters. Each part of the brain must be developed and put to work in its proper role, just like every military unit has a specific job. No part of the brain can replace another, just as infantry can't perform the tasks of artillery.

Hamerton said, "Discipline begins with the desire not just to do our best with the skills we have, but to reach the best we could have if we commit to proper training." No matter what you think about military readiness, mental readiness is just as important—and obvious. But are we willing to face the hard work, drills, and sacrifices that true training demands? Mental readiness means persistent, focused effort, sometimes without visible rewards—only the inner satisfaction of staying true to our ideals, meeting the chances to serve, and acting on our deepest beliefs.

Mental discipline is essential before true intellectual success can be reached. While no amount of willpower can make a genius out of an ordinary brain, a will that fully controls and trains the mind creates efficiency, culture, happiness, and success in whatever field the mind is suited for.

A worthy goal for any person is to master and conquer their own mind. Breaking a person's will—especially a child's—is against nature. But to control and guide one's own mind by will is perfectly natural. Alexander the Great, one of history's greatest conquerors, once wept when told there are infinite worlds, saying, "Isn't it sad that with so many worlds, we haven't conquered even one?" Alexander was a powerful man who conquered much of the known world but could not conquer himself. He died young after a long night of excess and self-destruction—showing how even a strong mind can be ruined if undisciplined.

Similarly, Hannibal, the great Carthaginian general, was defeated not by armies but by uncontrolled desires. Despite his military genius and victories over harsh conditions, he was overcome by luxury and pleasure. From youth, he dreamed of defeating Rome and was one of history's greatest strategists. But in the end, his will was weakened by unchecked physical appetites.

Success requires a strong will that commands the mind, guiding every thought and action with discipline. Only then can a person achieve true greatness and lasting achievement.

The Romans were angry with their leader, Fabius Maximus, called the Delayer, because of his careful and slow military tactics against Hannibal and his army made up of Africans, Spaniards, and Gauls. Yet, every time they ignored his plan, they were defeated. What the Roman soldiers couldn't win by force was eventually done for them by the bright, lively climate of Italy. Hannibal's army was destroyed by disease, he lost sight in one eye, and later, as a hunted fugitive in Asia, with no hope of escape, he ended his own life with poison.

Mark Antony had great natural talent but lacked the willpower to control his desires and focus his energy on meaningful, positive goals for himself and others. In his youth, he showed reckless behavior. While serving as Deputy Governor of Italy, he wasted time on wild excesses. After Julius Caesar's murder, Antony became one of three rulers of Rome. But in 41 B.C., he fell under the spell of Cleopatra, spending time and energy with her instead of serving the empire. His will weakened by indulgence, he behaved extravagantly and gave away kingdoms to Cleopatra. Eventually, in 32 B.C., the Senate took away his power and declared war on Cleopatra.

When Cleopatra realized her forces couldn't win, Octavian suggested she kill Antony. Cleopatra, who had been Caesar's lover and had killed her own brothers to stay in power, tricked Antony into joining her in a tomb, saying they would die together. Believing she had already killed herself, Antony took his own life. He died broken and defeated, his life full of promise wasted by a weak will. Though hardship had once pushed him to great achievements, success led him to give in to temptation and destruction.

Vitellius, Roman Emperor for just one year, was neither ambitious nor clever. He became emperor thanks to soldiers who enjoyed his wild parties and generosity, but his weakness soon destroyed discipline and order. Vitellius was lazy, self-indulgent, and controlled by two military commanders who used him for their own selfish goals. His army entered Rome like a wild mob, causing chaos, violence, and immoral behavior. When Vespasian, a strong man from humble origins, became emperor, Vitellius was captured, mocked, and brutally killed. His reign had weakened Rome's morals and power because of his selfish lifestyle.

Alexander the Great's weak will led to his early death, wasting a life full of great power and promise. Hannibal's weakness ruined his purpose despite his brilliance. Antony's will was too weak to resist pleasure and focus on duty, turning him into a traitor and a broken man. Vitellius's weak will destroyed himself and his country, turning Rome into a reckless, undisciplined mob heading toward ruin.

A person's will is a constant expression of their freedom. Without free will, morality loses meaning. Every thinking person knows freedom is real. Will is shown in the choices we make and the purpose behind our actions. The most important parts of will are Free Choice and Purpose. A strong will is not always good—it can be used for wrong aims—but a weak will is always a flawed, incomplete part of a person's character. The first rule of virtue is strength; the second, just as important, is having a clear purpose that drives us toward our ideals.

True success depends on a strong, focused will that directs every step toward meaningful goals and the betterment of ourselves and the world. W. H. Thomson said that it is the powerful, personal will that truly makes the brain human. A mind that thinks by choice, not just by automatic reactions, leads a life with purpose.

The gift of a personal will is one of the greatest privileges given to every person—it is a test of how much a person can shape themselves. This will gives us the greatest possession of all: self-control. Self-control means the ability to guide ourselves, to hold back impulses, and to choose our own direction.

A complete and successful life is one where the true inner self always holds the steering wheel, guiding the person through the rough and unpredictable seas of life toward a higher, meaningful goal.

To steer toward the wrong destination, or to switch between two opposite goals—whether in morals or life direction—or to sometimes act with purpose but at other times drift aimlessly with the crowd, is to live a life of mistakes and failure. Eventually, such a life faces the natural law of cause and effect—nature's fair balance of action and consequence.

As an old saying reminds us:

"There is no wrong done by anyone that will not come back,
Its return may be twice as bad, and no skill can stop it.
Just like mist on the earth turns to rain from the sky,
The evil done to others falls back on the doer.
It is the law of life that wrongs bring retribution; It never fails,
though punishment may take time to come."

Success means mastering your will, steering your life with steady purpose, and living in harmony with this natural law of cause and effect.

Chapter-4

Great Minds and Strong Wills

Great progress is born when a person's will becomes free, focused, and fearless. This chapter shows how strong will and clear purpose can rise above poverty, doubt, tradition, and opposition to reshape history itself. Through the lives of determined pioneers, it reveals how unwavering resolve turns vision into reality and individual effort into lasting benefit for humanity.

Emerson once said, "There can be no real driving force except when a man becomes his will, and his will becomes him." A man's power to change the world and bring humanity closer to a greater ideal comes from the free human will—one that is not tied down by tradition, blind customs, or the opinions of the crowd. Instead, it is brave and persistent, guided by reason and inspired by the spirit of creation and progress. A strong and perfect will controls the body, leads the mind, and guides the moral self. The great achievements that stand the test of time were made by strong-willed people with clear purpose, working in harmony with the universal will. Success comes only when will and purpose supply the steady energy needed to break new ground, overcome obstacles, and do pioneering work.

Take Christopher Columbus (1451–1506) as an example. His father was a poor wool worker in Genoa. By age fourteen, Columbus worked as a laborer, then as a dockworker, sailor, and at nineteen, a weaver. Yet by twenty-eight, through self-teaching, he was making maps and charts. He believed the world was round and dreamed of reaching Asia and India by sailing west, opening a new sea route that was easier and freer than the old caravan trails. Despite many setbacks, in 1492 Columbus sailed west with three small ships and a crew of eighty-eight, many of whom were criminals or outcasts. He battled storms, fear, superstition, and mutiny. But his powerful will won over every challenge. He discovered the islands of the New World—a land that would change history forever. Though he thought he had reached Japan, Columbus proved the earth was round and found a new continent. His strong vision and will, undeterred by the opposition of people and nature, gave the world a new future.

Richard Arkwright (1732-1792), inventor of the spinning frame and founder of the modern factory system, also shows the power of will. Born the youngest of thirteen children to poor, uneducated parents in England, Arkwright grew up without schooling. As a boy, he apprenticed to a barber—a humble start for a man who would later lead the Industrial Revolution. Despite barely being able to read or write, Arkwright had imagination. He understood the value of a good spinning machine and refused to spend his life shaving faces. Working sixteen hours a day, he devoted extra time to learning. His wife even smashed his first working model, begging him to return to barbering. But Arkwright's will and determination never wavered.

He faced harsh criticism. Townspeople feared his machine would take their jobs and attacked him, destroying his belongings. Forced to flee for his safety, Arkwright kept working, believing in himself until others did too. His health was weak, but his spirit was strong. He won recognition and wealth and was knighted for his contributions to industry.

Carlyle described him perfectly: "In shaving and beard lathering, amid confusion and hardship, this man had ideas in his rough head—spindles, wheels, and machines—that he finally brought to life through great struggle. What a historical wonder he was: awkward, enduring, inventive!" This unremarkable, poor boy with a plain appearance became the man who gave the world the power of cotton and the factory system. With a strong will, clear purpose, and far-reaching vision, Arkwright changed the world.

Both Columbus and Arkwright dreamed big—but they worked hard and never gave up. Their success came because they refused to be stopped, even when others mocked or attacked them. Their strong wills made their dreams real and brought lasting benefit to humanity.

Martin Luther (1483-1546) was the son of a miner from Thuringia. He had to beg and sing for food just to attend school. Hardship and struggle were constant companions for this poor boy. He grew up not surrounded by luxury, but by tough, real life. Luther was a rough, ordinary man with a plain and strong face. He wasn't dreamy or deeply spiritual, but he had a powerful will—once he decided on something, no force could change his mind. When Luther spoke out against Tetzel's indulgences—papers that promised forgiveness for sins—he didn't plan to rebel against the Pope or the Church. Yet, his stand sparked the Reformation and helped build Protestantism.

Luther's nature was common and rough; he believed in devils and sometimes struggled with hallucinations worsened by alcohol. Still, he was brave and persistent. When his beliefs were challenged, he stood firm, no matter what. On April 16,

1521, as Luther entered Worms, a messenger begged him not to go into the city where his death was planned. Luther answered boldly, "Tell your master that even if there were as many devils in Worms as roof tiles, I would still enter." Whether you agree with Luther or not, his final words at Worms show noble courage: "Prove me wrong; I cannot take back what I said. It is neither safe nor wise to act against one's conscience. Here I stand; I can do no other. God help me."

These powerful words show a will that is strong and a purpose that is noble. They remind us of Socrates, the greatest thinker of ancient times—a man even greater than Luther. Socrates was firm and true to his beliefs, but he also showed love, kindness, and respect for others' opinions. When falsely accused, Socrates did not try to please the jury with excuses. His life was full of meaning, his will was like steel, and his principles never wavered. He said, "Men of Athens, I honor and love you, but I will obey God rather than you. Decide my fate, but I will never change my ways—even if I must die many times." After being sentenced, he calmly said, "No harm can come to a good man, in life or after death. Now it is time for me to leave, I to die and you to live; but only God knows who will have the better fate."

Socrates could have escaped death, but he stayed true to his values. He did not compromise with his unfair enemies, and because of this, his memory has inspired people through the ages. His student Xenophon said no one ever heard him say or do anything wrong or disrespectful. Socrates humbled himself to connect with ordinary people so he could lift them higher. His self-control was absolute, and he was satisfied with very little. "To want nothing," he said, "is divine; to want as little as possible is the closest to divine life." A fellow philosopher once joked that even a slave would run away from him, but his admirer Alcibiades said, "I have no shame, but I am ashamed when I am with Socrates."

No one can fail to be inspired by Socrates' freedom of mind, reasoning skills, humility, determination, and strong character. He was "so devoted to the gods that he did nothing without asking their guidance; so just that he never harmed anyone; so temperate that he chose right over pleasure; so wise that he never made mistakes in judging good and evil—in short, the best and happiest of men."

Musonius Rufus, a Roman philosopher of the First Century, was another man of strong will and purpose. He lived a life of virtue and kindness, earning respect from friends and foes alike. He ignored applause, saying, "If you have time to praise me, I am wasting my words."

One student said Musonius spoke as if he were always answering for his actions, pointing out everyone's faults clearly. He was like the famous Roman Cato, trusted for his honesty and respected for his fearlessness. When Roman armies fought near Rome, Musonius urged soldiers to choose peace, virtue, and goodwill—showing great courage. He was so respected that even Emperor Vespasian kept trusting him when other philosophers were banished. Musonius had a powerful and steady will. He believed true virtue is not just theory but something we live by every day.

In modern times, Ulysses S. Grant (1822-1885) is a great example of strong will used for success. As a young man, people called him "Useless Grant." He left the army in 1854 and tried many jobs, often failing. Some even said he was a failure. But when the Civil War came, Grant found his purpose at the Battle of Shiloh. Whether or not he drank alcohol, he had an iron determination that outweighed his faults. He always stuck to what mattered. When the battle looked lost, he calmly said, "Never mind, boys, we'll win tomorrow." When asked what to do next, he replied simply, "Keep on fighting."

Grant became the Union's savior with his clear judgment, bravery, and steady determination. President Lincoln praised him for his "cool persistency of purpose," saying, "When he gets a grip, nothing can shake him." His famous "Hands Off" order showed his strong will: "I intend to fight it out on this line if it takes all summer."

Even George Washington had many military failures, but he never gave up. He kept fighting, crossed icy rivers, and won victories against all odds.

James A. Garfield had a clear purpose and a strong, energetic will. He lost his father when he was only eighteen months old and grew up in the backwoods of Ohio without many opportunities for schooling.

As a boy, he did chores like chopping wood, driving a team of animals, and farming. He worked hard to earn a few pennies to help his mother. Despite his tough life, Garfield was determined to grow his mind and create a future as a scholar and teacher. By the time he was sixteen, he worked as a canal boat driver, studying books whenever he could. Later, he became a janitor at Hiram College, where he swept floors, rang bells, and did any small job needed to stay close to learning. He graduated with high honors from Williams College and achieved his dream by becoming a teacher, and later the head of Hiram College.

But Garfield's ambitions went even higher. At twenty-nine, he became a State Senator. At thirty-two, he was made a Major General in the army.

A year later, he joined Congress. When he was forty-eight, he was elected to the United States Senate, but before taking his seat, he was elected President of the United States. This great rise—from ringing bells in a small school to the highest office in the country—showcases the power of a determined mind and strong will.

As the poem says, "The heights by great men reached and kept Were not attained by sudden flight; But they, while their companions slept, Were toiling upward in the night."

Nathan Hale (1756-1776), a young patriot from Connecticut, was full of energy, passion, and strong will. His deep love for his country and his fellow citizens gave him purpose. He was once part of a small group that bravely captured an English supply ship right under the guns of a British warship. Later, he was captured while spying for the American cause. Despite his youth and noble spirit, he was cruelly hanged as a spy in the first year of American independence. His final words still inspire us today: "I only regret that I have but one life to lose for my country."

Sydney Carton, a memorable character in Dickens' "A Tale of Two Cities," lacked strong will in much of his life. Though brilliant, he wasted his talents and struggled with his own weaknesses. Yet, when given the chance to show love and sacrifice, he rose nobly to the occasion. He gave his life so others could live freely and happily. His last words were filled with hope and peace: "It is a far, far better thing that I do than I have ever done; It is a far, far better rest that I go to than I have ever known." Carton's story shows the true nobility inside a person—the divine spark in human nature—and hints at what he could have achieved if he had directed his will daily toward a life of strength and virtue.

The great willpower and vision of Columbus did not bring him personal wealth, but they created opportunities for future generations to enjoy freedom, prosperity, and happiness. Arkwright's strong will quickly brought benefits to his country, himself, and eventually the whole world. Socrates' courage and firm will contributed to mankind's mental freedom, and his influence lives on even though he died as a martyr for free thought.

Luther fought against religious corruption and commercialism, sparking a movement far bigger than himself. Musonius taught people to think for themselves, improve their character, love others, and refuse to harm anyone under orders.

Young Garfield was determined to educate himself and become a teacher. His focused mind and strong will led him beyond his original dreams. Nathan Hale gave all his energy to fight for his oppressed country, only regretting that he could not give more. Grant's determined will ended slavery and united a nation. Washington's courage and unshakable purpose won independence and built a great land of freedom and opportunity.

All these men had energy to act, the mental strength to see a clear vision and goal, the wisdom to choose the right path, and the will to stay on that path despite obstacles, setbacks, and opposition. These qualities, combined with kindness, honesty, and tolerance, create a rare and complete life—the highest form of human achievement and the true meaning of success.

Chapter-5

Mental Discipline and the Moral Self

True power does not come from talent alone, but from a trained mind guided by a strong will. This chapter explores how self-knowledge, moral balance, and mental discipline awaken the soul's deeper strength. It shows why knowing oneself is the foundation of wisdom, ethics, and true freedom—and how inner mastery shapes character, purpose, and meaningful life.

Ovid once said, "It is the mind that makes the man, and our strength lies in our immortal soul." But really, it is the will that shapes a person—the will is the expression of the soul's energy, which defines our true self. Cicero called the cultivation of the mind "food for the soul." As the mind is trained, educated, and developed to serve under the guidance of the soul's will, the soul grows stronger and more effective. Well-trained mental abilities are to the soul what limbs and senses are to the brain. The more a person develops their mind fully, the more powerful their soul becomes in the world. The human brain is simply the tool that lets the soul work in harmony with the greater Cosmic plan. "There is one mind common to all individual men. Every man is an inlet to the same and to all of the same."

The most cultivated minds are the most moral. Although history shows some geniuses were immoral, here we speak of well-rounded, enlightened minds—not those with limited or unusual talents. Developing the mind and practicing mental discipline lead to self-control. Too much excess, on the other hand, destroys intellectual strength and "weakens the springs of the mind." Plutarch shared that two phrases were inscribed at the Delphic Oracle, perfectly suited to human life: "Know thyself," and "Nothing too much." He added that all other lessons depend on these. The wisdom of knowing oneself is clear and accepted in theory, yet most people only understand it abstractly, not personally. They apply it to humanity as a whole, but not to their own self. They nod in agreement but do not live it.

Most people's attempts at self-analysis are a joke—a mockery of true inquiry and a sign of the ego's dislike for truth. To truly know yourself, you must compare your present self with your ideal self—the better, truer self seen from a higher, divine perspective. As St. Augustine advised, you must "go up into the tribunal of your conscience and set yourself before yourself." Here, the soul acts as judge, the will as law, and the mind as the prisoner.

Protagoras and the Sophists believed that to know truth, one must look beyond the deceptive senses and rely on reflection and reason. Yet they made a mistake by saying no universal truth exists and that truth depends on individual opinion. When Protagoras said, "Man is the measure of all things," he only considered the changing individual, ignoring the unchanging spiritual element common to all. He wrongly claimed that goodness, justice, and truth depend on personal taste, making individual whims the final judge. His skepticism weakened the old beliefs and paved the way for the spiritual philosophies of Socrates, Plato, the Cynics, and the Stoics. But Protagoras failed to see that human reason is essentially the same in everyone. As Weber said, "Men hindered him from seeing man."

Socrates picked up where Protagoras left off. Though he claimed to know nothing, he believed there is something absolute that can be known—man himself, as the Delphic Temple advised: "Know Thyself." We may never fully understand the universe's nature, origin, or end, but we can know what we should be, the purpose of life, and the highest good for the soul. This knowledge alone is real and useful because it is the only true knowledge. Without ethics, there can be no serious philosophy.

Socrates moved from the individual to the universal, discovering beneath humanity's many faces one unchanging human nature. In a time of confused opinions, he found the true, lasting conscience of humanity—the law of the mind. He brought order to intellectual chaos. He believed moral ideas are central to humanity, that every mind contains truth, and that education does not create knowledge but awakens what already exists inside us. As Weber noted, the deep connection between knowledge and will forms the core of Socrates' philosophy. The more a man thinks and understands, the better he acts. Our moral worth grows with our insight. Virtue can be taught, no one is bad on purpose, and evil comes from ignorance. We can all reach knowledge of the highest good through our inner spirit, which guides us with an infallible inner sense.

Socrates gave people an absolute, unchanging standard to judge themselves—one unaffected by personal whims. He opposed the popular belief that good and evil are relative and that success is the only rule for judging actions. Socrates stood for intellectual freedom and urged people to reason, think deeply, and train their minds. He encouraged self-examination—judging our thoughts, words, actions, and motives with honesty and care.

Shinto Shrines in Japan stand out because they have almost no objects or tools for worship. Instead, a simple mirror hangs in the sanctuary—this is the most important item. When a person stands before the shrine to pray, their own reflection appears in the shining mirror. This act of worship reflects the ancient Delphic command:

"Know Thyself." For both the Japanese and early Greeks, self-knowledge is not about knowing the physical body or mind, but about understanding our moral nature—the true inner self. The Japanese say their temple mirror symbolizes the human heart, which, when calm and clear, perfectly reflects the image of the divine.

Following "Know Thyself," the next natural command would be "Use Thyself," because knowledge alone is meaningless if it does not lead to action. Marcus Aurelius, the wise Roman Emperor, wrote in his private meditations, "Remember how long you have delayed these things, and how many chances the gods have given you, yet you have not taken them. Now you must realize the universe you are part of, and that your time is limited.

If you don't use this time to clear the confusion from your mind, it will be lost forever."

This great emperor, who worked sixteen hours a day to rule justly and peacefully, believed true greatness comes from living honestly, knowing yourself fairly, regularly examining your actions, and following what you know to be right—no matter what others think or do.

Wisdom means not only understanding what matters most but also acting on that understanding. Sir Thomas Browne said, “A man truly lives as long as he acts according to his nature and uses his abilities well.” An old philosopher advised, “If it is not right, don’t do it; if it is not true, don’t say it.” We can improve this advice by turning it positive:

“If it is right, do it; if it is true, say it.” Holding back, making excuses, delaying, and avoiding action are some of humanity’s greatest problems today. The world doesn’t just need people to avoid wrong—what it really needs is the active, joyful, and timely doing of good. Negative advice was valuable in the past, but today we need encouragement to take posi tive steps: Man, not only Know Thyself, but also Use Thyself.

The mind needs the will to spark interest. When the will drives attention, it leads to learning. Knowledge then helps us see opportunities to serve, giving the mind reasons to act. Knowledge and laziness cannot live together; only false knowledge can tolerate inactivity and stay useless. A person who thinks with clear purpose will speak, act, and live with that same purpose—showing the true power of life.

The other Delphic command, "Nothing too much," reminds us to develop all parts of ourselves evenly. No part or quality should grow too much at the expense of the whole. Natural, balanced growth is what we should aim for. Mental discipline, guided by a strong will and working with the universe's forces of life, brings sanity, balance, calmness, and natural goodness. Many things are called evil only because they are uncontrolled. Undisciplined mental power wastes energy, causing mediocrity and mistakes. Any virtue pushed to an extreme becomes a vice—just as a normal rain nourishes life, but too much drought or flood destroys it. Moderate sunshine in a temperate climate brings comfort, while extreme heat or cold can kill. We feed our bodies to stay alive, but overeating harms rather than helps. Too little food kills, but so does eating too much. Exercise keeps us healthy, but no exercise weakens the body, and too much exercise leads to exhaustion or even death.

Fear of illness, which weakens the body and mind, is an error. But so is ignoring hygiene, refusing precautions, and neglecting science's advice to protect ourselves and others. True virtue lies in the middle way. Aristotle expressed this well: virtue is the balance between two extremes, both bad. For example, courage lies between cowardice and recklessness, truthfulness between false modesty and bragging, and generosity between greed and wastefulness. He also said that the "true gentleman" is one who avoids extremes.

Pindar, a Greek poet from the fifth century B.C., praised Lampon of Aegina for "seeking the middle path in thought and action," echoing Hesiod's earlier words: "Keep a middle course; the right measure in all things is best." Anyone extreme in their passion or effort shows unbalanced virtue that has lost its strength and purpose. A miser, once a careful saver, has lost sight of what really matters. A madman is often someone whose mind has wandered too far from truth, losing connection with solid, reliable reality—his thoughts flying off course into confusion.

Balanced mentality, guided by freedom and discipline, leads to a clear, strong, and harmonious life.

Plato (427-347 B.C.), known as "the Homer of the Philosophers," was one of the brightest Greek thinkers and the greatest follower of Socrates' ideas. He taught that there are four main virtues: Wisdom (the reasoning part of the soul), Courage (the emotional part), Soberness (the desire or appetite part), and Justice—the highest virtue that gives each part its proper role. Because Justice keeps everything balanced, it leads to the idea of moderation. As E. Vernon Arnold explains, even virtues have limits in how strong they should be and where they should be used. If any virtue goes too far, it turns into a vice that borders on it. The ideal person, then, is moderate—calm, thoughtful, and self-respecting—who feels deeply but never loses control. Still, this ideal is below the higher goal of a life devoted to philosophical thinking and reflection.

Growth and development are essential parts of life and evolution. But growth should never break the natural laws of the universe. It should be about organizing and directing raw forces into harmony and useful forms. When growth in one area happens at the cost of others, it leads not only to imbalance and ugliness but also to failure and death. Life itself is growth, but growth that follows the laws of nature—a continuous movement toward a higher ideal. Wherever there is life, there is growth; when growth stops, decay and decline begin.

Some say virtue is always good and vice always bad, and that you can't have too much goodness. Ancient philosophers taught the idea of the "mean," meaning we should avoid extremes, just as the Delphic Oracle advised: "Nothing too much." But today, people often see only one side of this truth. What does "goodness" really mean? We call a skilled machinist, a loving father, or a talented violinist "good," but we also call a dog"good" and even say we have "good food" or "good tools." Goodness means being or acting according to one's true nature. Everyone and everything has a purpose, and goodness means performing that purpose well—living in harmony with natural law and growth.

The ancient Greeks called this natural power "Phusis." It is the force that shapes everything in the world, helping things grow toward their highest potential. As Gilbert Murray said about Stoic philosophy, "Phusis shapes every living thing into a more perfect form—the seed into an oak tree, the puppy into a skilled hunting dog, the wild tribe into a civilized city." Call it Phusis, Evolution, or God—this power pushes us to live according to our true nature, not simply or primitively, but in tune with the spirit that drives the world's growth and progress.

Goodness means living and working with these cosmic forces as they move toward achievement and perfection. To be good, a person must use their talents well and do their duties properly. Ignoring mental abilities or refusing to develop and use them is wrong. A lazy, inactive mind cannot be good. At the same time, pushing growth too far in one direction while neglecting other parts of the mind is also wrong because unused abilities weaken and go against natural law. True goodness means using your gifts fully for the benefit of humanity and civilization. It requires knowing what really matters and understanding universal laws.

The world moves forward by law. Humanity will grow toward perfection and the ideal human being. Every cause produces an effect as an exact and unchanging response. Success is the true measure of goodness, and morality only feels satisfied with success. A good farmer does not grow poor crops. A good engineer does not build weak buildings. A good sailor avoids dangerous rocks. A good doctor does not harm patients. A good cook makes food that nourishes. Likewise, a good person lives a good life. Henderson said, "Failure is just another word for immorality, and human failure means human immorality." He also said that "the lack of health, wisdom, accomplishment, and kindness is a moral failure."

In short, freedom of the mind means growing, balancing, and using our true nature wisely and well to live rightly and succeed in life.

When we consider a person alone—not including their ancestry—we must recognize that some health conditions and physical limits are inherited. Everyone's mental abilities, talents, and tendencies come with certain natural limits. Still, most of a person's illness or physical problems happen because of their own choices, especially when they don't develop or use their mind fully. A person is acting immorally if they block or ignore their natural drive toward improvement—the very force that gives human life meaning and greatness. Even a physically perfect body is not moral if the mind, soul, and social feelings are neglected. A brilliant scholar who lacks love and sympathy is not truly moral. Perfect morality does not exist as a fixed point; living morally means being active, thinking clearly, making decisions, overcoming difficulties, and achieving difficult goals.

God is not a random or changing being who breaks the natural order. Instead, God's will is an unchanging law—"What a man sows, that shall he also reap." Goodness comes from using one's talents well, living and growing according to nature, and following a straight path toward the goal without getting distracted by tempting but wrong directions, even if society says otherwise. The world's opinions often change. What is seen as good today may be called bad centuries later. Many virtues praised long ago are now criticized. But the Law of Nature—the Law of God—never changes. It is eternal and the one true power in life. Human laws, by contrast, are just temporary guesses at truth, used until something better comes along.

What disappoints many people about the world's ideas of goodness is how fake and shallow they often are. Rochefoucauld said, "We are so used to hiding our true selves from others that we even hide from ourselves—our virtues are often just hidden vices." Smart, thoughtful people often get discouraged in their search for true goodness because they see many false morals pretending to be real. This leads some to doubt whether true moral goodness exists at all. An old Roman once bitterly said, "Virtue, I worshipped you as a real god, but in the end I find you are an empty name."

True virtue only comes from real goodness and truth. It is not something that grows slowly through repeated purification, like refining a chemical. Virtue appears fully formed, like the goddess Minerva born from Jupiter's head. An action is either good or it is not. If it follows the Cosmic Law and expresses our higher nature—the purpose for which we were made—then it must be good. "Let us never grow tired of repeating that good and great things come only from a good and great purpose." To call an action virtuous, the motive behind it must also be good. Sadly, many actions that look good on the surface fail this test. Any act that is fake, selfish, harmful, or thoughtless is not inspired by goodness. "Nothing damages genuine value more than skillful counterfeits." To be genuine is to be good.

The world needs the whole person—the real, complete person—and always at their best. Haddock said, "Nature's law says a person must try to make the most of themselves in every way that does not harm their soundness. This is the first law of holiness—wholeness—soundness." When this principle guides behavior, it becomes the service the world desperately needs. The world is ruled by those who serve it well. The successful servant is the true king. What humans call goodness may sometimes be wrong, but goodness, as measured by Cosmic Law, is an absolute and unchanging truth. Therefore, goodness means fully using the natural, self-developing power within us.

Mental development is both a moral and practical force. The happiness that comes from achieving and using one's powers well is the fair reward for effort. A true worker uses their brain and talents for the joy of work and fulfilling their purpose. They do not worry about what happens after death or hope for rewards in another life.

They know that living according to nature, using their talents fully, and doing their best now brings happiness here—and that this happiness will not lessen beyond this life. The effective mind does not work to gain a future payout like an investment; instead, its reward is the satisfaction of living rightly in the present. And beyond this life, true happiness depends on activity and achieving worthy goals.

Gilbert Murray said, "The essence of goodness is to do something, to labor, to achieve some end." For goodness and happiness to last forever, the processes of the world must continue or be replaced by others—likely more complex than we can imagine.

Life is like a game of chess. Our task is to play this game well, following the rules and using the pieces we are given. Whether we have many pieces or few, we must understand the value and moves of each—King, Queen, Knight, Bishop, Rook, and Pawns—and use them wisely to achieve the best possible results. The great creative power of life may have given us a strong set of pieces, or mostly pawns; none of us likely starts with the full set of sixteen.

But our real duty is to make the most of what we have and play the game fully. Since everyone's starting position is different, we cannot judge people simply by how much they win or lose. "Life is not about holding a good hand, but playing a poor hand well."

Whether we succeed or fail by the world's standards doesn't matter as much as whether we have given our best effort and made full use of our gifts. Victory belongs to the one who fights hardest, not necessarily to the one who wins the world's praise. No one loses truly if their faith is strong and courage unbroken.

"To set the cause above renown, To love the game beyond the prize." Success means fully expressing yourself and all your natural talents to the world. Sometimes fate may clear the board and shock the player, but if we play honestly, earnestly, and with enthusiasm, our souls grow stronger. Our short lives—

sixty, seventy years—are just a brief flash compared to the endless progress of the spirit in the universe.

Huxley once said, "Imagine if it were absolutely certain that your life and fortune depended on winning or losing a game of chess. Wouldn't we all feel it was our duty to at least learn the names and moves of the pieces? Wouldn't we look down on anyone who grew up without knowing a Pawn from a Knight? Yet this is exactly how life works.

Our life, fortune, and happiness depend on knowing the rules of a far more complex game than chess. This game has been played for ages. Each man and woman is one player, and the chessboard is the world. The pieces are everything we see around us, and the rules are the laws of nature. The player on the other side is hidden from us. We know that player's moves are always fair, patient, and just. But we also learn, often painfully, that mistakes are never overlooked or excused. Those who play well receive great rewards, given generously by strength. Those who play poorly are eventually defeated—slowly, but without mercy."

So, are we playing life, or is life playing us? If a person only thinks about rewards—money now, heaven later—then life controls them. But if they work out of love and joy in doing, they truly play the game well. Playing for the game itself—that is happiness. All other rewards are just pleasant extras. Emerson said, "The reward of a thing well done is to have done it."

A person who avoids work, ignores chances, and operates by instinct rather than thought is like a Pawn on the board in life's great game. Such a person does only what is necessary, never all they can, and so drifts through a meaningless, empty existence. They brand themselves a Pawn, and the world takes them at their word. Until they are forgotten, a Pawn they remain.

Life is like any game that needs skill and faces challenges. James Tyson, the Australian Bushman Millionaire, was once asked about his success. He said his life had been a game with the harsh desert as his opponent. "I fought the desert all my life and won. I brought water where there was none, raised cattle where there were none, built fences and roads where none existed. Nothing can undo what I've done, and millions will benefit long after I am gone and forgotten."

Epictetus taught that if a man enters the game of life, he must prepare for the struggles he will face. He must be ready for setbacks. If he cannot face hardship calmly and wisely, he is like an athlete who quits after a single blow—showing cowardice instead of strength. Instead, he should say, "This is why I trained myself." For a thinking person and philosopher, life is like competing in the Olympic Games.

You must follow rules, control your habits, exercise your body at set times, whether hot or cold, and surrender yourself to your trainer as you would to a doctor.

In the contest, you might fall, hurt yourself, swallow dust, and still lose. But can you live as you do now—angry, undisciplined, unhappy—and call yourself a philosopher? No. You must watch yourself, work hard, control your desires, and give up much if you want peace, freedom, and calm.

In life, mental discipline, steady effort, and purpose are the keys to true freedom and success.

Life is a game we play with ourselves, with others, and with the world. It's a game of individuals and teams, all working within the great Cosmic

Plan that encourages achievement and growth. When we compete one-on-one, it's a test of many mental abilities—not just one skill, but a combination of strengths. For example, a golfer who finishes a round in 90 tries to improve to 88, then 86, always aiming to beat his own best score. In a tennis singles match, the goal is to outperform your opponent.

But in team sports like football or baseball, each player gives their best for the good of the whole team, putting personal glory aside. Every game has its mirror in life, and every person with passion inside wants to succeed, to improve, to win.

Confucius captured this idea perfectly when he said, "Every normal person wants to become superior—not only better than others but especially better than their own past self."

If Confucius lived today, he might admit that true "normal" people are rare. Today, many chase power and money, but not real inner growth or true excellence.

They want more money, more free time to waste, and more things to show off—things that others admire but are often shallow and artificial.

Confucius also said, "The superior person looks for strength inside himself; the ordinary person looks for it in others. The superior person's progress goes upward; the ordinary person's goes downward.

When you fully develop your own abilities and live by the rule of treating others as you want to be treated, you are on the right path. Self-development is the foundation of everything for everyone. If you neglect your roots, what grows from you cannot be strong or well-ordered."

Real intellectual and personal growth—the kind that comes from knowledge, goodness, and high human qualities—is like pushing a long wedge into the world. At birth, we start with the thin edge of that wedge, placed under the part of the world where we are meant to make a difference.

Throughout life, we must keep driving that wedge deeper and deeper, forcing our presence and influence into the world. The deeper the wedge goes, the stronger we become, the more impact we have, and the more work we can do. How far we push that wedge is a clear sign of our growth and success in the great school of life.

Chapter-6

The Eternal Quest for Freedom

Human history is filled with struggles for freedom, yet true freedom has never depended on power, wealth, or position. This chapter reveals how real freedom is born within the mind and will, not in external conditions. Through the wisdom of ancient thinkers and the life of Epictetus, it shows that even in chains, a person can remain free—if their thoughts, values, and inner will cannot be controlled.

Throughout history, the loudest cry of mankind has been for freedom. In early times, this meant freedom from the physical control of others. Yet, even then, people often enjoyed more freedom of thought and individuality than those living in the early Christian and medieval periods. Before religious leaders held absolute power, figures like Medicine Men and Pagan Priests influenced society, and superstition was widespread. Still, a person could often think and speak freely, much more than their later medieval ancestors. If someone truly wished, they could experience full mental freedom.

True mental freedom began when early philosophers like Thales, Xenophanes, and Pythagoras—whom Aristotle called "Physicians" to separate them from earlier "Theologians"—moved gods and myths into stories and started explaining nature with logic and reason. Could there have been a greater freedom of individual thought than what these ancient Greek, Roman, and Eastern philosophers enjoyed, surrounded as they were by a rigid and unthinking society?

In those times, social rank or worldly power did not control a person's freedom of thought or expression. For example, Marcus Aurelius was a Roman Emperor, while Epictetus was a crippled Greek slave. Despite being poor, maimed, and owned by a cruel master who broke his leg, Epictetus knew what true freedom meant.

He said, "Look at me—I have no city, no home, no possessions, no servants. I sleep on the ground, have no family or wealth, only the earth, sky, and a worn cloak. But what do I want? Am I not free from sorrow and fear? Have you ever seen me fail in my desires or fall into what I avoid? Have I blamed God or man? Have I ever accused anyone? Did you ever see me with a sad face?"

Though trapped in a broken body and a despised slave, Epictetus was free in soul, mind, thought, and speech. He rejected materialism and the worship of outward things. He spoke boldly and freely whenever he wanted. "There is only one thing that is truly ours—our will—and no one can take that from us," he said.

Once, he added, "You can imprison my body, but not even Zeus can control my mind." His philosophy was deeply practical and showed a high, ideal sense of morality. He strongly believed in justice and mental freedom, hating the chains of mindless traditions and complicated, confusing arguments.

During the time of Imperial Rome, many people born into slavery rose to positions of power and respect. In the large households of wealthy Romans, talented young slaves had amazing chances to learn and climb the social ladder. Education was encouraged everywhere to help youth develop their abilities and take on greater roles.

Plato said we can't find a king without slave ancestors or a slave without royal ancestors. An ancient writer even claimed that many Roman slaves were better educated than their masters.

Emperor Claudius chose his ministers from among his freed slaves, which caused the Roman aristocracy to mock him, but it greatly improved the government of the Roman Empire. Vespasian, who ruled as Roman Emperor from 70 to 79 A.D. and was the father of Emperors Titus and Domitian, came from humble roots.

Born in 9 A.D. near Reate to a plebeian tax collector, he lived simply and set an example that shamed the luxury-loving Roman nobles. Vespasian was a straightforward soldier with strong character and clear goals.

He worked hard to restore order in a morally weak empire and focused on the welfare and prosperity of his people. He welcomed criticism, famously saying, "I will not kill a dog just because it barks at me."

Cornutus, an African philosopher and writer (20–66 A.D.), started life as a slave in the house of the Annaei family and became the teacher of poets Persius and Lucan. Phaedrus, a Roman writer of fables and a contemporary of Christ, was once a slave and later freed by Augustine.

Epictetus rose from physical slavery to become a free and respected philosopher. Terence, the famous playwright, was brought to Rome as a Carthaginian slave. His master, Terentius Lucanus, a Roman senator, freed him because of his literary and philosophical talents. Terence became close to learned Roman nobles like Scipio, Laelius, and Furius Pilus. Despite a short life—likely ending around age twenty-five—Terence's work earned him great fame.

Marcus Porcius Cato, known as "the Elder" or "the Censor" (234–149 B.C.), came from a plebeian family and was raised as a farmer, a profession looked down upon at the time. He became a great statesman, philosopher, and soldier, always opposing luxury and living simply.

When asked why many Romans had statues built to honor them while he, more worthy, had none, Cato replied, "I would rather people wonder why Cato had no statue than why he had one."

In earlier Greek times, Persacus of Citium (300–243 B.C.), a noted philosopher and general, began as a personal servant to Zeno before becoming his close companion. Cleanthes (331–232 B.C.), Zeno's successor as head of the Stoic School, came from a humble background. He was the Stoics' poet and theologian and wrote a famous "Hymn to Zeus," asking for wisdom to guide human life away from ignorance and shame.

Iphicrates, a great Athenian general in the early fourth century B.C., was the son of a poor shoemaker. A brilliant military mind, he invented new fighting equipment and won many battles. When Harmodius, who claimed noble descent, insulted him for his low birth, Iphicrates replied, "My nobility seems to begin with me, but yours ended before you."

Solon (638–558 B.C.), the Athenian statesman and lawmaker, was born poor and had to support himself from childhood. Despite his father's reckless spending that sometimes left him in great hardship, Solon's genius prevailed. He became one of the most learned and respected men of his time and is remembered as one of the Seven Sages of Greece.

Hesiod, from the 8th century B.C., the father of Greek didactic poetry, was a simple shepherd. Cyrus the Great rose from humble origins as a soldier and statesman to become the founder of the Persian Empire. In 538 B.C., he was crowned King of Babylon and ruler of many lands. Some ancient accounts say he was the son of a poor bandit; others say he came from a poor shepherd family. All agree he started from a modest Persian tribe and rose to build one of the greatest empires in history.

Diogenes was born the son of a dishonest swindler and was sold as a slave in Crete to Xeniades, a man from Corinth. When asked about his skills, Diogenes said he knew only one trade: ruling men. He wanted to be sold to someone who needed a master. Diogenes taught the importance of self-control and virtue. To him, true virtue meant pursuing what is good and lasting, while avoiding shallow physical pleasures. He believed society's artificial customs clashed with truth and goodness, and that true morality meant returning to nature, reality, and simplicity. Diogenes showed a godlike strength of will and full control over his desires. By an odd coincidence, he died at ninety years old on the very day that Alexander the Great, aged thirty-three, died from a life of excess.

At the Isthmian Games, Diogenes once asked Alexander for just one favor—that his military victories would not block Diogenes' view of the sun. Alexander replied, "If I were not Alexander, I would want to be Diogenes." This raises the question: who was greater—the emperor or the slave; the soldier or the philosopher? The brilliant mind destroyed by drunken excess, or the grander mind that controlled desires and used inner strength for the good of self and society? The man who killed in passion, or the man who loved all others? The conqueror of much of the world who never conquered himself, or the slave who mastered himself completely?

After Alexander died, his empire, built on violence and ambition, quickly fell apart. It caused great suffering and left no lasting good. But Diogenes influenced the world forever with his high ethical ideals, deep sympathy for others, and honest search for truth. More than four centuries later, Epictetus said of him: "Diogenes was kind and loved all people. He willingly suffered for mankind.

All the earth was his home. When he was captured, he did not miss Athens or his friends. Instead, he grew close to the pirates and tried to help them. Even after being sold, he lived in Corinth as freely as he had in Athens. This is how freedom is won." Diogenes, the slave, not the proud Alexander, truly conquered the world.

In times when slavery was common and men owned others, young people could still rise through hard work, talent, and determination. Many came from the lowest ranks to become intellectual leaders or powerful figures. So, today, with freedom, no one should say the door to progress and success is closed to anyone who has the talent and the drive to develop and use their abilities persistently.

Marcus Aurelius, the noble pagan emperor, and Epictetus, the noble slave philosopher, offer the highest examples of Roman stoicism and ancient wisdom. Epictetus showed that a slave could live a life of great dignity despite harsh conditions, through mental freedom. Marcus Aurelius, known as "the Philosopher on the Throne," proved that even an emperor born into privilege could live simply, with virtue, service, and humility. He practiced justice mixed with mercy and kindness every day.

Marcus Aurelius said, "What guides a man? Only one thing—philosophy, which means love and search for truth. It means keeping your spirit free; doing nothing without purpose; being honest and sincere; not needing others to act for you. If you work seriously and calmly on what lies before you, following reason and keeping your inner self pure, as if you had to return it at any moment; if you hold firmly to this, expecting nothing and fearing nothing, content with your present actions according to nature, speaking truth boldly, then you will be happy. No one can stop this."

Xenophanes of Colophon, born around 580 B.C. and called the "Voltaire of Greece," was a free thinker who lived a long life. After the Persian conquest of Ionia, he refused to submit and became a wandering minstrel before settling in Elea, Italy. Xenophanes wrote many controversial works, criticized the gods of Homer's stories, and insisted that truth must be known by all. He said, "There is one God, greatest among gods and men, not like a mortal in body or mind." His ideas were considered heresy by many but Greek society did not persecute religious thinkers, except in Athens.

Athenians did not like free thought or open argument about truth in religion. While other Greek cities welcomed debate, Athens was proud and resistant. They disliked outsiders calling their sun a hot iron ball or their gods mere poems. When a prophet with strong but untrained imagination criticized the city's religion, Athens punished such speech as a crime. Philosophers like Damon and Anaxagoras were banished, the great Pericles fought to save Aspasia, Socrates was sentenced to death, Plato often had to be careful what he said, and Aristotle preferred freedom outside Athens to limited freedom inside.

Despite this, the Greek world generally tolerated different beliefs. An Oracle at Delphi said, "Each man's proper religion is that of his fatherland." Freedom of thought, inquiry, and tolerance were valued ideals.

Socrates, born in 469 B.C., taught that all popular ideas should be tested by reason. Every question should be met with an open and free mind. No one should accept opinions just because they are popular or come from authority. Socrates' skill in reasoning inspired his followers to become wiser and better people. He promoted careful thinking, understanding the small in relation to the large, and aligning oneself with divine will. This prepared a person to face the world with self-control, strong reasoning, and a genuine wish to do good for others. Socrates showed the world how to live a life full of action, kindness, patience, and self-control. His character and ideas have inspired people for over twenty-three centuries and will continue to influence many more generations to come. Cicero said, "Socrates brought philosophy down from the heavens into the homes and cities of people, making them question life, morals, and what is good and evil." Seneca wrote that Socrates "brought all philosophy to focus on moral questions and said that the highest wisdom is to know the difference between good and evil."

Socrates led by example in doing his duty with courage. As a soldier, he fought bravely in three battles. As a judge, he stood firm, even under pressure, refusing to give in to angry crowds. When Athens was controlled by the harsh Thirty Tyrants, Socrates boldly opposed their unjust orders. When he was sentenced to death, though he could have escaped easily, he chose to stay, saying that to flee would break the laws of his country.

After seventy years of a meaningful life, Socrates died by drinking poison hemlock rather than compromise his principles. He rejected political tricks and refused to bend his strong will to falsehood. Though not a martyr by choice, he was a victim of politics and jealousy. The charges against him were that he did not believe in the city's gods, introduced new gods, and corrupted the youth. His accusers were a poet, an orator, and members of a patriotic party. At his trial, Socrates said, "If you want to free me on the condition that I stop searching for truth, I thank you, but I will obey God, who I believe gave me this task, rather than you. As long as I live, I will never stop doing philosophy. I do not know what death is—it may be good, and I am not afraid. But I do know that it is bad to abandon my post. I prefer what may be good to what I know is bad." Socrates defended the unbreakable right of individual conscience and the absolute freedom of thought. He valued open discussion and criticism as the best way to find truth. "In me," he said, "you have a tough critic, always pushing you, questioning your beliefs, showing you how little you really know. Talking about these things every day is the greatest good for humans. A life without such questioning is not worth living."

Zeno, a philosopher born in Cyprus in 336 B.C. (the same year Alexander became king), was a student of Socratic ideas. He studied under Crates of Thebes and later founded the Stoic school of philosophy. Stoicism taught that the individual alone truly exists, that virtue is the highest good, and that a wise person—even a poor beggar—is truly a king. Zeno believed the ideal society must include the whole world, built not on changing opinions but on solid knowledge and unchanging truth. He believed this ideal would come through the use of human reason and practicing philosophy. To Zeno, virtue was knowledge, and knowledge was reachable by all humans.

Alexander the Great showed that trying to unite people by force and conquest was impossible. Zeno's vision was of a world state where no one would say, "I am from Athens or Sidon," but, "I am a citizen of the world."

Socrates and Diogenes had already said they belonged not to a city or class but to the whole universe, where all races and classes are united by brotherhood.

Zeno said such a world state would follow laws set by nature, not by human customs. It would have no temples or statues because God cannot be pleased by gifts or worship. There would be no courts because all citizens would be just and harm no one.

This world community would not be held together by force or politics but by goodwill and love—a divine power working for the common good. Zeno believed that narrow-mindedness and selfishness, especially among philosophers and leaders, delayed the coming of this perfect state.

Eager to learn from everyone, Zeno once visited the home of Stilpo, another philosopher. When Crates tried to force him back to his own school, Zeno said argument, not violence, should decide. "Philosophers' best handle is by the ear—try to convince me, and I'll follow you. But if you use force, my body may stay, but my soul will be with Stilpo."

Zeno taught that "Example is stronger than words" and "Virtue is the only good." He believed reason, or the divine mind (Logos), rules the universe and should rule the individual too. Those who live by a single, harmonious principle have divine favor and a balanced life. Those who live with conflicting goals are unlucky. Virtue, found in living consistently with nature and the cosmic order, is enough for happiness—it needs no outside support. Therefore, life should be lived "in agreement with nature."

The Academy was founded in Athens by Plato in 380 B.C. About a century later, around 300 B.C., Zeno started his own school. His followers were first called Zenonians and later Stoics, named after the "Painted Porch" where Zeno taught, a place decorated with paintings by Polygnotus. At the same time Zeno was developing his ideas, another famous school was started by Epicurus (341-270 B.C.) in his gardens in Athens. Epicurus taught that pleasure was the goal of life, combining this with the atomistic philosophy of Democritus. His materialistic teachings were the opposite of Zeno's, so naturally, their schools often clashed. Around 270 B.C., Arcesilaus, once a student alongside Zeno, became head of the Academy and openly challenged the teachings of both Zeno and Epicurus.

Interestingly, despite these deep disagreements between the Academy, the Porch, and the Garden schools, Athens' political life remained peaceful. The citizens enjoyed watching the schools compete for students and influence, and welcomed the many foreigners who came to Athens for education. They showed great respect to the school leaders. Zeno, for example, was honored with the keys to the city, a gold crown, and a bronze statue—though he and Cleanthes, the religious poet-philosopher who followed him, both declined Athenian citizenship to show respect for their birthplaces.

Zeno died in 264 B.C. at age 72. The city of Athens passed a special resolution honoring him, a tribute that stands in sharp contrast to the way Socrates was condemned 135 years earlier:

"Zeno, son of Mnaseas from Citium, has spent many years in the city pursuing philosophy; he has been a good man in every way; he encouraged the youth who came to him toward virtue and self-control; he showed by his own life the teachings he preached. Therefore, the people of Athens commend Zeno and crown him with a golden crown for his virtue and temperance. They will build him a tomb at public expense. Five citizens will be chosen to oversee this. This decision will be engraved on two pillars—one at the Academy and one at the Lyceum—so all may see that Athens honors good men both in life and after death."

While the charges that Socrates faced were stronger than anything Zeno was accused of, the city had come to see the value of philosophy. This decree can also be seen as a late recognition of Socrates' greatness.

The mental and religious tolerance seen in Athens during Zeno's time, and across much of the ancient world before and during Socrates' life, was also reflected later in the Roman

Empire. In 155 B.C., the leaders of three great philosophical schools spoke to large, open-minded audiences in Rome. Diogenes of Seleucia represented the Stoics, Critolaus the Peripatetic school founded by Aristotle, and Carneades the Academy. Their deep thinking, freedom of expression, and clear logic impressed many Roman thinkers, even as the empire still honored traditional pagan gods.

Throughout history, philosophical debate has been a path to truth. Superstition, rigid theology, and unquestioned authority have long been dark shadows that block clear thinking and the full use of human reason.

Cleanthes of Assos (331–232 B.C.) took over as head of the Stoic school after Zeno. A man of humble background, trained through hardship and endurance, he was a worthy successor to Socrates, Diogenes, and Zeno. It is said that he would fetch water at night so he could study philosophy by day. Cleanthes often used poetry to clearly express his ideas and reach people's hearts. He advised, "Do not follow common opinion or rush to be wise suddenly. Do not fear the chatter of the many, for most have no true judgment or modesty. Among the few, you might find fairness and wisdom."

Chrysippus (280–206 B.C.), who succeeded Cleanthes as head of the Porch School, shared this distrust of popular opinion and honored the power of individual reason and freedom of thought. When asked why he had not studied with the popular philosopher Aristo, he replied, "If I had followed the many, I would never have become a philosopher."

The Stoic philosopher was expected to be well-trained both in mind and morals. Today, the world still needs such people. Under all conditions, a Stoic must speak only the truth—nothing less, nothing more. Arnold writes, "He could not hold back anything from his listeners, even if it offended their religious beliefs, patriotism, or sense of decency. He could not add a word just to appeal to their feelings or stir their anger in his favor. He always kept in mind Socrates' example during his trial."

The Stoic appeared before the public as a balanced, brave, and honest speaker, avoiding tricks, emotional appeals, and crowd manipulation. Gellius tells us that Diogenes, who greatly helped develop the Stoic style, was known as a quiet and self-controlled speaker.

The Stoics believed that philosophy often went against popular opinion, but as Cleanthes said, it was always in line with reason. Cicero tells us they taught six important ideas:

1. Only what is honorable is truly good.
2. Virtue alone is enough for happiness.
3. Right actions and wrong actions are equally clear.
4. All foolish people are truly mad.
5. Only the wise person is free; every fool is a slave.
6. Only the wise person is truly rich.

Before Stoicism became mixed with religious beliefs and strict rules, it was basically the religion of mental freedom—the freedom of the mind to think clearly and live rightly.

Far away in China, when the great teacher Confucius died at age 73 (479 B.C.), his last words were a sad reflection: none of the rulers then understood the true value of ethical philosophy. Though he died quietly and without honor, he believed his calls for mental freedom, truth, justice, hard work, self-control, moderation, and public service would one day deeply move humanity.

Emperor Tsin Shi-hwang tried to destroy Confucius' writings by fire, but they survived and continue to inspire people to be free and noble. Confucius clearly explained the heart of true morality and honesty of mind—the kind of thinking that never shuts the door to truth. He said simply, "When you know something, admit you know it; when you don't, admit you don't—that is true knowledge."

Confucius taught that the power and freedom of the human mind are what set people apart from animals. But he warned that many waste this gift, while the "superior man" keeps it strong. He was free from following customs blindly or holding stubborn opinions. "He had no fixed ideas, no stubbornness, no selfishness." He believed the greatest joy comes from sincere and honest self-examination. Confucius even quit a political job because he refused to work with anyone so controlled by selfish desires that they lived an immoral life.

In India, Gautama Buddha, called "the awakened" or "the enlightened one," was a prince named Sakya Muni who taught obedience to reason and universal kindness. Some call Buddhism a religion of pessimism, but it was really a rebellion against tribal fights, rituals, and many gods.

Buddha shared his ideas freely and openly, without restrictions on his freedom of thought or speech. Buddhism grew strong because of its broad spirit and beautiful moral teachings.

Buddhism taught that happiness doesn't come from birth or status, but from a person's actions and thoughts. It rejected the idea that Brahmins (priests) were the heavenly aristocracy and instead became a faith of justice, morality, and freedom for all people. In a famous sermon at Benares, Buddha described the "Eightfold Path" to end suffering: Right Belief, Right Aspiration, Right Speech, Right Action, Right Living, Right Effort, Right Meditation, and Right Self-Control.

The Dhammapada, a Buddhist text, contains teachings that if followed, could end wars and many evils.

For example, "Hatred never ends by hatred; it ends by love. This is an ancient truth. Let a man conquer anger with love, evil with good, greed with generosity, and lies with truth."

In India, the Gymnosophists, often Buddhist monks, taught philosophy with courage, kindness, humility, and high ethics. Plutarch tells a story of how Alexander the Great captured ten of these Indian philosophers, who were said to have inspired a revolt. Alexander tested them by asking difficult questions, punishing the one with the worst answer each time.

When asked if there were more living or dead, one said, "The living, because the dead no longer exist." When asked which land or sea produced the largest animals, the answer was "The land, because the sea is part of it." Asked which animal is the cleverest, the reply was "One that man has not yet discovered."

When asked why he made Sabbas rebel, another said, "So Sabbas might live or die with honor." Asked whether day or night came first, the answer was "The day, by one day." When asked how to be most loved, one replied, "By being strong but not feared."

To the question of how a man could become a god, the answer was "By doing the impossible." Asked which is stronger, life or death, the reply was "Life, because it can endure great suffering." Finally, asked how long a man should live honorably, the answer was "As long as he thinks life is better than death."

Alexander was amazed by their free and quick thinking and let them go free. Though poor, almost naked, and rejecting luxury and comfort, these philosophers were powerful leaders because they used their minds to the fullest.

In ancient pagan times, independent thinking saved lives and original ideas were respected. Later, in the Christian era, opposing the accepted authority often meant persecution, suffering, or death. Christ died as a martyr for truth, 432 years after Socrates. He was killed by religious fanatics, even though the law found "no fault at all" in Him. Christ was a simple carpenter called by a higher purpose to leave his workshop and share the gospel with the world. He was a man of the people, with little formal schooling, but his wisdom came from deep spiritual understanding, beyond the senses.

After the death of this greatest prophet and simplest philosopher, an era of Mental Repression began. Over time, people allowed their minds to be controlled by strict dogmas, and their souls to be chained. History shows us that knowledge grew when minds were free to explore and question. In modern times, since restrictions on thinking have eased, knowledge has grown at an incredible pace. From the sixteenth century until today, almost every major event has been linked to humanity's fight for freedom of thought and release from the mental slavery of early Christian and medieval times.

As the historian Bury said, "It took a long time to realize that forcing people to think a certain way is a mistake—and even now, only part of the world truly understands this. This is perhaps the most important lesson humanity has learned."

Throughout the Christian era, there was a constant battle between authority and reason. Authority used violence, laws, punishment, and social pressure to control people, while reason's only weapon was argument and discussion. Reason refuses to accept unfair restrictions, because doing so would betray its very nature. It will never submit to mental slavery but insists on absolute freedom in all areas of thought and experience. The greatest achievement of modern civilization is the freedom to think and speak openly. Though sometimes abused by careless or extreme minds, this freedom is essential for social progress and human development. However, many have fought blindly for so-called freedom of thought, chasing illusions instead of real mental freedom, because they were stubborn or poorly informed. Sadly, during the Christian era, every freedom gained seemed to come with some new form of mental slavery. History is full of examples where those who fought for tolerance later became intolerant themselves. Today, mental slavery still exists—often more harmful than physical slavery ever was. At every point in history, those who truly cared about reason and independent thought have been a small, lonely minority. As Spencer noted, "It often seems the majority want to get through life using as little thought as possible."

If we do not use our mental abilities, develop our brains, and practice reason, we become puppets on life's stage—controlled by outside forces, suggestions, and false beliefs. We accept others' opinions without questioning or checking them, and fail to use our own minds to judge their truth. This mental laziness harms our growth and leads us away from our true potential. It's important to understand the difference between true freedom of thought and forcing others to accept our beliefs. Also, freedom of thought is not the same as freedom of action. While thought mainly affects oneself, actions can impact others' freedom and happiness and sometimes need rules for the good of society.

A free person is one who uses their mind under the control of their own strong will—someone who thinks and reasons for themselves and forms their own opinions about life. As it's said, "The revealing of thought brings people out of slavery into freedom." True freedom is found in the persistent search for truth and in openly expressing it, living in harmony with nature and universal laws. As Payot wisely said, freedom means understanding both the outer world and one's inner self. Without these two, true and balanced personal growth is impossible.

Chapter-7

The Cost of Passionate Will

Great strength without self-mastery can become a danger rather than a blessing. This chapter examines how uncontrolled will, vanity, and lack of inner balance can undermine even the most extraordinary abilities. Through the example of Alexander the Great, it shows that true greatness depends not on conquest alone, but on discipline of mind, character, and moral control.

Alexander the Great (356-323 B.C.) is often seen as a man with incredible strength, unstoppable will, and unmatched ability. But in reality, he was an unstable person with immense but uncontrolled power. He was burdened by a vanity that bordered on madness, and his belief that he was a god made him unpopular with the simple Macedonians. He could not handle criticism or honesty, and when drunk or challenged, he often exploded into uncontrollable fits of rage. His personality is much like Stevenson's "Dr. Jekyll and Mr. Hyde"—full of extremes and contradictions: strong yet weak, noble yet cruel, with both kindness and cruelty without limits.

Alexander had a brilliant but chaotic mind that often drifted away from focus. His will was too weak to discipline his thoughts and shape a balanced, steady, and positive character. If Alexander had managed to control his life with a stronger will, he might have lived a longer, more fruitful life and changed history even more. The world might have looked very different: Italy might never have united under Rome; Carthage might have stayed Greek; the Roman Empire might never have existed; and Latin could have remained a simple rural language, eventually replaced by Greek.

His great victory—conquering Persia—was made possible largely by his father, Philip II, a practical genius. Philip became head of the Greek Confederation through a mix of bribery, clever politics, and military power. He trained an excellent army and prepared a plan to "avenge the ancient wrongs of Greece." Alexander inherited his father's throne, army, and mission to conquer Persia. But Alexander was restless and fearful during his father's last years, worried that Philip would get all the glory and leave him nothing to achieve. Because of Philip's second marriage and the rise of Cleopatra's relatives, Alexander's claim to the throne was threatened, and many suspected Alexander had a hand in his father's murder. Before becoming king, Alexander killed an innocent infant brother and cousin to secure his place.

Alexander's campaign was historic, but his biggest worry during it was that he could not control his own soldiers and people. The closer his men were to him, the more they saw his unstable, unpredictable nature and selfishness, which made them unhappy and restless. The historian Grote said Alexander "had none of that sense of correlative right and obligation which characterized the free Greek."

Alexander was painfully aware that he was simply reaping the rewards planned by others, and that he had not surpassed the boundaries set by the great Persian kings, Cyrus the Great and Darius. The famous story that he wept because there were no more worlds to conquer is false. Many lands—Arabia Felix by the Red Sea, gold-rich Ethiopia, Carthage in the West, silver-rich Spain, Sicily (which Athens failed to conquer), Rome and other Italian cities, and even far-off places like Northern Europe, China, India, and Africa—were still free and untouched by his empire. Many of these places defied him, even though he had sworn to erase the word "barbarian" from Greek language, relying mainly on his fierce Macedonian soldiers, hardy and wild mountain fighters.

As a young man, Alexander was quick and agile. His father once encouraged him to run in the Olympic race, but Alexander scornfully replied, "I would if there were kings to race with me." When Darius offered peace through arbitration, Alexander answered, "The earth cannot bear two suns, nor can it tolerate two kings." He was not a patriot but a selfish egoist. He fought not for Greece, but for Alexander himself. One historian said his goal was to make Greece Persian, not Persia Greek. This explains his kindness to the conquered Persians—he needed their loyalty to keep his empire strong and continue his ambitions. Alexander liked the natural obedience of the Persians, something weak and shallow men often crave. He made everyone bow before him and declared himself the Son of Jove, claiming the Oracle of Jupiter Ammon in the Sahara as proof.

When Alexander's uncle invaded Italy and was defeated, Alexander sarcastically said his uncle had "fallen upon the chambers of women, but he on the chambers of men." This insult was repeated by Alexander's close friend Clitus during a drunken celebration in Samarcand. Alexander, overwhelmed by anger, killed Clitus, his trusted companion who once saved his life. By murdering his closest friend in a fit of rage fueled by drink, Alexander destroyed himself—his weak and inconsistent will could not control his wild mind and desires, ultimately breaking his health and causing his early death.

Alexander, who claimed to be a god, was not immortal enough to withstand the damage caused by alcohol and his own unstable nature. After his death, he was embalmed and placed in a golden coffin, buried with great ceremony in his city of Alexandria. But isn't it a bitter irony that later, one of his own generals' descendants, Ptolemy, took Alexander's body from the golden coffin, melted the precious metal for his selfish use, and reburied Alexander in a plain coffin? As Marcus Aurelius wisely said, "Death makes Alexander of Macedon no different from his stable boy."

The story of Alexander—the man who appeared great on the outside but was deeply unstable inside—teaches us a powerful lesson about a weak will. Despite having great mental strength and potential, his inability to control and guide his powerful mind led to tragedy. Imagine high-pressure steam without a steady hand to control it—valves burst, springs lose their tension, and eventually, the whole system breaks down. Alexander's powerful mind and passionate energy, meant to drive the world forward, instead led to his early downfall.

Napoleon is often called the Alexander of modern times, but he had a much stronger will. However, Napoleon's will was directed by selfishness and error, driving him to gain power through bloodshed and arrogance. His rule was built on false pride and deceit—"false as a bulletin," as the saying went in his day. Whatever good qualities he once had were lost under layers of lies and cruel ambition by the time he became Emperor. He took the force unleashed by the French Revolution and used it for his own personal glory. Napoleon's goal was to start "his dynasty," worshipping self and ambition as gods. Carlyle said Napoleon wrapped his flawed self in "a cheap patchwork of theatrical paper and glitter, hoping to make it seem real." With a soul stained by violence and falsehood, Napoleon demanded a grand coronation from a democracy that had sacrificed half a million lives to end tyranny, as his general Augereau pointed out.

Napoleon believed that his strong will and grand appearance could fool everyone, crush the truth, and let him live forever glorified on a cloud of lies. But such a life is always short and fleeting—like a sudden blaze that burns bright for an hour and then fades away. Just as Alexander fought for himself and not for Greece or Macedonia, Napoleon cared more about

Napoleon than about France. France was great, but "was he not France?"

Alexander's life shows the dangers of a weak, unstable will—a personality torn by inner conflict. Napoleon's life shows the pain caused when a strong mind is twisted by selfish ambition and cruelty. The Duke of Weimar encouraged his friends, saying, "Be brave, this Napoleonism will not last because it is built on lies and injustice." Carlyle also warned that injustice brings terrible consequences. The more tyrannical forces like Napoleon's militarism oppress and crush the noble and divine parts of humanity, the stronger the world's backlash against such cruelty becomes.

Napoleon ended his life in exile on St. Helena instead of ruling the world as he dreamed. His real legacy to Europe was militarism—the worst curse born from revenge and greed. Until militarism is defeated like Napoleon was, the world will continue to suffer from the destructive mix of selfishness and falsehood that came from one powerful mind, forced down a path of evil by a will driven by ambition and cruelty.

Today, people sometimes call powerful businessmen or financiers "Napoleons," but this is often a mistake. Those who achieve success through hard work, focus, and strong will are truly great—if their purpose is good and benefits humanity. Calling such men "Napoleons" insults their true achievements. But if their ambition is selfish, built on lies, and they cheat or oppress others, if they believe might makes right and worship money above all, then the name "Napoleon" fits them—and the world would be better if such people were sent away, like Napoleon, to isolated exile.

There are far more "Alexanders" than "Napoleons" in the world. Few people have wills strong enough—and dark enough—to push themselves against their better nature like Napoleon did. Many have weak, unstable wills and minds that fluctuate. Anger and outbursts are common not only among the poor and uneducated but also among rulers and leaders. The more mental a person's work, the stronger their mind and will should become. But today's unnatural lifestyle, which often strains the brain at the expense of the body, leads to nervous tension and instability. Losing control of one's temper is a temporary return to a more primitive, less human state—almost a form of madness, breaking the rules of reason and universal law. Thankfully, mental effort also helps develop the will to control these nerves and emotions, helping us rise above these setbacks.

A truly great person is one who has a strong will that is wisely guided—someone who controls their mind like a careful engineer controls steam pressure and throttle valves. This careful control keeps the safety valves from blowing off and conserves energy, so inner power can be used for meaningful, productive work. Losing your temper is a sign of weakness. Passion, when uncontrolled, is crude and brutish. Explosive behavior is foolish, irrational, and wastes energy. Many people excuse outbursts as "righteous indignation," but much of this so-called anger only eats away at the mind and body. True anger, when it is justified, shows itself in calmness, steady determination, and real effort to fix problems—not in pointless shouting or venting frustration.

Passion, whether praised as a sign of virtue or blamed as a sign of vice, is actually a mistake—it weakens and drains a person. The first step to using your energy well is to stop giving in to loud, uncontrolled expressions of strong feelings. The next step is to stay calm inside, see things clearly and realistically, and refuse to be consumed by anger that only weakens your effectiveness. Real change begins when you learn to use your energy outwardly and constructively—to control and overcome problems with sympathy and clear purpose, instead of wasting strength on empty drama or bitter internal struggles. A strong, focused will rejects uncontrolled passion and outbursts of any kind.

When a will guides the mind toward higher truth and purpose, it must use all its strength wisely. It tightens the springs of the safety valve and carefully manages its power, directing it where it will do the most good. People like Alexander, who are ruled by passion, doubt, and mood swings, are difficult to work with in everyday life—but when they are in positions of power, they become a real problem. An "Alexander" in charge forces others to follow his ever-changing whims. There is only one right way to do things—and it is always his way, even though what he says on Tuesday often contradicts what he said on Monday. Alexanders crave the spotlight, but it must shine only on themselves. Like Nero of ancient Rome, they tighten or loosen control depending on their mood, rewarding or punishing others not based on fairness or truth, but on their own selfish, narrow views or sudden impulses.

Truth, goodness, and what is right are clear, constant, and eternal. Yet an Alexander's will is so changeable and unpredictable that what he praises one day, he rejects the next. He demands total obedience because, after all, he believes he is perfect—the "Son of Jove." Such a man insists that everyone under his power become servants to his ego. As a result, great minds and talents, which should help the world move forward, are instead trapped and crushed under his rule.

In contrast, a truly great leader helps others grow. He works to develop the hidden and obvious strengths of everyone around him—from assistants to the humblest workers. His will is strong and steady, aimed at a goal in harmony with universal truth. His ego is set aside for a higher purpose that seeks the greatest good for all. He is not fanatical but balanced; not a follower of fads but a wise, expanding conservative. His decisions are based on justice, not wild emotions, passions, or whims. His honor is built on unchanging truth, not shifting policies. He is never overly critical or tricky but expresses himself with clear logic and calm reason, combined with tolerance and human kindness.

Such a leader is not perfect but always improving. He understands his limits and is content if he is moving in the right direction, using all his abilities and inner strength to lift himself and others toward greater truth and usefulness in the world.

Napoleon fought for democracy but wanted a crown as his reward. Cromwell fought to free people from oppression, to end false worship of empty symbols, and to bring honest representation to the people. Yet, after becoming "commander-in-chief of all forces," Cromwell used his army to become almost a king himself, opposing free voting and dismissing parliaments. He fought against a weak, corrupt king for democracy, only to rule as a harsh dictator with both sword and Bible in hand. This shows how strong men sometimes build proud empires on shaky foundations, fooling their followers with the appearance of truth while lulling their own minds to sleep with grand words.

The human will is often unsure and changeable, caught between truth and error, good and bad, life and death. A strong will aimed in the wrong direction opposes everything noble and lasting. But a well-guided will, like a compass pointing to the stars, strives and grows toward divine truth. A soul with such a will—whether its mind is complex or simple—is worthy of being called "A Son of Jove," a glorious title for mortal man inspired by greatness and purpose.

Chapter-8

The Quiet Call of Opportunity

Opportunities pass quietly through every life, often unseen and unnamed. This chapter reveals why success belongs to those who stay alert, prepared, and ready to act when the moment appears. It shows how missed chances never return, why early action matters, and how focused awareness turns passing moments into lasting achievement.

The world of opportunity is open to everyone. Life flows past every person, offering at some time or another a chance to use their natural mental abilities. When we use these abilities, we contribute something—big or small—to the meaningful work of humanity. Every person, in some way and at some time, can make use of their talents. But Fate, like a mysterious force, doesn't announce these chances with fanfare. Instead, it often seems to enjoy quietly trapping those who are blind to it. Only a few people hear opportunity loudly, like a trumpet blast. Most have to search carefully, learn to recognize their chance quickly, grab it, and hold on as it passes like a shadow or through a mist. Sometimes, when we are busy with daily life, a figure named Opportunity—old as time itself—may knock loudly at the door of our mind, announcing the arrival of a chance toward something great. But more often, he slips by silently, like a ghost, leaving no sign of his visit. As the old saying goes, "Opportunity comes with soft feet." It takes a keen, artistic sense to feel and understand when opportunity is near.

Opportunities are not clearly marked, and they never come with labels showing their value. No two chances are exactly the same. Once an opportunity is missed, whether because we ignore it or don't act, it is lost forever—it will never return. The chances we get in youth don't come back in middle age or old age. Success in early life builds the foundation for greater achievements later. The Japanese have long understood this truth, believing that honor gained early grows stronger with time, and that "an opportunity missed in youth will not return in old age." There is a story from the famous siege of Osaka where a young warrior begged to be placed at the front of battle but was held back because of his youth. When the castle fell, he cried bitterly. An old advisor tried to comfort him, saying, "You have many years ahead; there will be many chances to prove yourself." The boy looked sharply at the man and said, "How foolish! Will my fourteenth year ever come again?"

To seize every opportunity and make the most of changing circumstances, our minds must always be focused where insight lives. We should live fully in the present with all our creative power, while also keeping a clear vision that looks ahead like a searchlight through the fog. Constant watchfulness, combined with understanding and energy ready to act, is the key to true, lasting success. Most people must shape their own futures, and this can only happen through preparation, hard work, and quick action when opportunities arise. As Rochefoucauld wisely said, we should not waste time trying to create chances, but instead be ready to use those that come our way. We cannot make opportunities appear out of nowhere, but we can search for them and, by catching invisible threads others miss, turn them into valuable paths. Those who do this prove to be wise and successful.

Opportunities surround us all the time. They whisper or shout in everyone's ear and pass by every person's door in some way and at some time. Those who are alert and energetic respond and succeed. Those who are deaf or hesitant stay inactive and slide from passivity into failure. Saint Beuve spoke of Joseph Joubert, a talented French thinker who left little behind, saying he lived in the space between "The time has not come yet" and "The time has passed." Chances came to Joubert but slipped away because his spirit to act and the right moment did not align. Coleridge, a man of genius, left behind many unfinished works. Charles Lamb mourned him, saying he "left about forty thousand treatises on Metaphysics and Divinity but not one completed."

No one should be so upset by lost chances that it hurts their ability to act now. Nor should anyone ignore present chances while waiting for something better in the future. The past can teach us, but living in the past or future is dangerous. Small or seemingly unimportant opportunities taken now prepare us to handle greater ones later. Many believe that important chances come only as sudden, dramatic revelations—like angels appearing or voices heard by saints. Imagination may create such visions, but true chances are found in the everyday paths of all people—kings and peasants, scholars and the so-called uneducated, rich and poor alike.

An old Italian saying goes, "If not everyone can live on the town square, everyone can feel the sun." Happiness, service, and achievement come in degrees, but all can reach their highest possible efficiency according to their own natural abilities, no matter how big or small their role may seem. Every person has potential, as Ulysses said, that should not be left dull but made to shine. Talents shine brightest when opportunity calls us to use and develop them in service to the world.

Homer mocked inactivity, saying life is about doing, not just breathing. Life is motion. We are always moving from past to future, and at the door of the present, each of us is given a chance and a challenge: to make our lives count in the grand scheme of things. The past is gone forever, and its chances will never come back—but it lives on as the source of the future. Ignoring the past leads to laziness and indifference now, since bad habits grow fast and trap us. Constant awareness, careful watchfulness, and joyful timely action are keys to success and worthy achievements. Taylor said, "Looking back, life is full of missed chances," but it is equally true that focusing on now and what is ahead offers amazing chances to those who see and are determined to act.

Jules Payot noted that some people let chances for real success and joy slip away because it is too much effort to grasp them. Such people live empty lives. St. Jerome jokingly compared them to wooden soldiers who always hold their swords raised but never strike a blow. Life's law is clear: effort is needed for results. Work is the true path to growth and lasting success. When Polycrates asked the Delphic Oracle how to find treasures buried by a general on the battlefield, the answer was simple: "Turn every stone." When Newton was asked how he could understand difficult science so clearly, he said, "By persistent thought and work." A modern scientist, asked if his inventions were the result of inspiration, said yes—but only if inspiration includes concentration and hard work. Cervantes said, "Diligence is the mother of good fortune."

It doesn't take much skill to begin a task or even to grab some opportunities, but it often takes real energy, persistence, and courage to finish the work well. As Plutarch said, "No real man ever wet clay and left it, hoping bricks would form by chance." Usually, it's wise to entrust the start of any good project to Argus, the one with a hundred eyes, who watches carefully for chances to serve. Then, the end should be given to Briareus, the one with a hundred hands, who pushes the work forward with energy and care. We shouldn't judge a person's usefulness by how many things they start or opportunities they take, but by the things they complete. For example, the telephone became truly practical because Bell gave one last, crucial turn to a screw. The world needs finishers—people who can add the final, important touch to whatever they do.

It's easy to do what we must and to act when pushed, but the true test of a person is not just doing what is required, but willingly taking on tasks they choose themselves. Goss said, "A man is not fully a man who doesn't do some things with his teeth clenched and his face set." True achievement comes from overcoming resistance. Life full of power and service is not a holiday; it demands taking on challenges, using the will to overcome, and struggling within the soul to win. There is an old saying: "Men are like salmon—only the living swim upstream; the dead just float downstream."

When people succeed, they often praise their own greatness but blame fate or the gods when they fail. One of the most common traits we inherit from our ancestors is the nearly obsessive desire to blame others—people, events, or circumstances—for our troubles and mistakes. "Adam blamed Eve; Eve blamed the serpent." Homer tells us that humans foolishly blame gods for their failures when in truth it is their own blindness that causes most pain. The gods say, "Men blame us for the bad things, but really their own foolish hearts bring more sorrow than fate ever planned." The cause of failure lies not in the stars but inside ourselves. Emerson said that at every moment, it is the person alone who determines their position in life.

As Shakespeare put it:

"Our remedies often lie within ourselves, Which we mistakenly give to heaven; the fatal sky Only pulls back our slow plans when we ourselves are dull."

Alexander the Great believed fate favored him but died young because he ignored nature's laws. Cicero trusted luck but was murdered in revenge. Caesar told a scared sailor during a storm not to fear because "Caesar and his fortune are on board," yet fate didn't protect him from assassination. Napoleon often spoke of destiny but died alone and broken in exile. Wellington, his conqueror, never believed in luck. He prepared carefully, planned for surprises, and faced emergencies with steady mind and action. At the Battle of Waterloo, he said, "This is hard pounding, gentlemen—but let's show them who pounds hardest and longest," never mentioning fate or fortune. Madison C. Peters said, "Bad luck is a man with his hands in his pockets, waiting to see what happens. Good luck is a man with his sleeves rolled up, working hard to make things happen."

Those who claim they never had a chance usually mean they had no special advantages over others. But chance and advantage are very different. Real chances for success, growth, and character do not depend on being born with a "silver spoon." The walls of the temple of immortals are filled with the names of men who had "no chance" in the eyes of society. The greatest heroes of history were often poor men who fought hard to be heard and to share their message. The challenges they faced made them stronger, sharper, and braver—even though many became victims of prejudice as they fulfilled their important roles and earned their place in history.

If it weren't for the brave thinkers and workers who used their minds freely and stood alone against tradition, we would still be living in prehistoric times, "wearing rough skins and fighting with stone hammers." Although progress since then is less than many believed before World War I, any advancement beyond savagery is due to developing and using our mental powers and accepting some part of Cosmic Truth.

The faults of our modern civilization come from error, lack of true freedom, worship of appearances, and neglect of the inner self. Blind loyalty to tradition and weak-minded habits have turned men into geese in thought, parrots in speech, and sheep in action. War and violence are born from ignorance, destroying progress and killing the noble, cultured, and immortal parts of humanity.

Every person has many chances to develop and use their natural talents—if they truly want to. The path to lasting success and true greatness is paved by the work of those who "had no chance," as seen by lazy and thoughtless society.

Shakespeare, the greatest poet, was a poor boy who worked holding horses. Albrecht Durer, a great German artist, was one of eighteen children born to poor parents. Andrea del Sarto, one of Italy's finest painters, was the son of a poor tailor and had to start working at age seven to support himself.

Immanuel Kant (1724–1804), the famous philosopher from what is now Germany, was the son of a saddler and grew up poor. He was physically weak, had a curved chest, a deformed right shoulder, and later even lost his sight. Despite these challenges, by age thirty-one he was a university student. He lived a strict, highly disciplined life with great regularity. Although poor and sickly, Kant developed a powerful mind that influenced the whole world. He never traveled more than forty miles from his hometown of Königsberg, yet his ideas reached everywhere. He carefully used all his physical energy under the control of his brilliant mind and strong will.

William Murdock (1754–1839), a British inventor and engineer, was the son of a poor millwright. Despite "having no chance," he was the first to make coal gas usable for lighting, invented the long D slide valve, and created the oscillating engine. Mozart (1756–1791), born to very poor parents, was a child prodigy and admired in royal courts for a time. Yet, he died in a pauper's grave, his funeral shameful to the Court and society. Mozart's impact on music is immeasurable. Beethoven (1770–1827), the greatest composer of his time and the founder of modern orchestral music, was born into severe poverty. His father was a violent drunkard, and Beethoven suffered physical hardships, including deafness, worsened by neglect during childhood. Verdi (1813-1901), the famous Italian opera composer, was the son of poor shopkeepers but rose to become Italy's greatest musical genius.

Sir Humphry Davy (1778–1829), the celebrated English chemist, was the oldest child of a widow left in difficult financial situations. At sixteen, he worked for an apothecary and taught himself a wide range of subjects. He made many important discoveries and became a man known for his broad interests and kindness. The poet Coleridge said if Davy had not been the leading chemist, he would have been the greatest poet of his age.

George Stephenson (1781–1848), known as the father of the steam locomotive, was the son of a miner. As a boy, he herded cows and later worked in a coal mine. At seventeen, he could neither read nor write. Through hard work, Stephenson created his own "chance." He started attending night school at eighteen, developed his talents, and became a powerful force in industrial history. Alongside engineering and science, he enjoyed farming and gardening, which enriched his mind and contributed to his success.

James Hargreaves, who improved the spinning jenny, was an uneducated weaver from Blackburn, England. His fellow workers once destroyed his models and forced him to leave home. Like Richard Arkwright, Hargreaves was born and raised in poverty and ignorance. Yet both men, along with a "pot-bellied Lancashire barber," made their chances and changed the world forever. John Dalton (1766–1844), the English chemist and founder of atomic theory, was the son of a poor weaver. Despite the hardships of poverty, his strong will and determination helped him become one of science's greatest minds.

Elias Howe (1819–1867), the sewing machine inventor, was born in Spencer, Massachusetts. At sixteen, he left farm work to labor in a factory. His years of research were full of poverty and discouragement, but he never gave up. His wife's support was crucial in his ultimate success. Michael Faraday (1791–1867), the famous English chemist and physicist, was self-taught. The sickly son of a poor blacksmith, he apprenticed as a bookbinder as a boy. Faraday had "no chance" but fought against fate and obstacles, achieving great breakthroughs that helped mankind harness natural forces for good.

Robert Fulton (1765–1815), the American engineer, was born to very poor Irish parents and worked for a jeweler in Philadelphia in his youth. By taking control of his fate and believing in himself, Fulton became a great engineer. He built America's first successful steam vessels, experimented with submarines, and invented machines for spinning flax, making ropes, and polishing marble. Fulton was a man of many talents, including landscape and portrait painting.

Charles Goodyear struggled for years to make rubber useful. His family went hungry, neighbors mocked him, and many thought him insane, but he kept going and finally succeeded. Samuel Morse said, "I will take the lightning Franklin captured and send it flying around the world on a wire." Everyone laughed at this idea, calling him a "crank." A Congressman even said, "That old fool wants a law to stretch a wire between Baltimore and Washington so fools can talk forty miles apart." But Morse's invention wrapped the world in a web of instant communication.

Alexander Graham Bell faced similar ridicule when he suggested the telephone. Chauncey M. Depew dismissed it as a "toy for children."

The American sleeping car, once mocked as "Pullman's Folly," was another invention first laughed at. The railway system itself was once called absurd; critics couldn't imagine a train moving faster than a stagecoach.

Imagine if those who mocked George Stephenson's early locomotives had to tour today's modern railways, all thanks to the man they once mocked in Parliament.

One sarcastic question asked, "If a train goes nine miles an hour and a cow gets on the track, wouldn't that be awkward?" Stephenson replied calmly, "Yes, very awkward—for the cow."

These stories show that many great minds began with "no chance." Yet through persistence, hard work, and strong will, they created opportunities and changed the world.

Thomas Carlyle (1795–1881), the British essayist and historian-philosopher, was the son of a poor mason. He grew up in a large family with very little money, so his parents could not give him any help. Jean Francois Millet (1814–1875), the famous French painter, was born to a poor peasant family.

As a boy, he worked long and hard in the fields. Yet, his close connection to nature and deep love for its beauty later showed through his amazing paintings. Millet said that seeing pictures in an old Bible inspired him to paint what he had seen during his workdays—even while others were asleep.

John Tyndall (1820–1893), the British scientist, was born poor and had no early advantages. What he did have was a strong, unbreakable desire to do something meaningful. Despite many challenges, he devoted himself to study. He became a powerful teacher and an original engineer. Alongside famous thinkers like Darwin and Wallace, Tyndall helped bring modern science into the world's accepted thinking.

Handel, the great composer, learned music on an old clavichord hidden in an attic.

The strings were muffled with cloth so no sound could disturb the people in the house. Handel could only practice secretly during the night. The world agrees that Handel "had no chance" to learn his art, yet even blindness and illness did not stop him from creating incredible music.

America is known as the land of opportunity. Countless stories tell of poor boys who worked hard and smart in this free and fair society to become famous. Success isn't about wealth but about doing something valuable and lasting for the world and others. Some of America's richest men are not remembered as truly successful because fame and money alone don't show true creativity or goodness.

Abraham Lincoln (1809–1865) was a great American who seemed to have "no chance" to leave a mark on the world. His father was a lazy carpenter-farmer who couldn't read or write. Lincoln grew up in a rough log cabin in the wilderness of Indiana.

Life was hard, and his community was simple and poor. Yet, even as a boy, Lincoln showed the spirit of mental preparation. He sat on the cabin floor by firelight, reading and saying, "I will study and prepare myself, and someday my chance will come."

At nineteen, Lincoln worked on a flatboat traveling to New Orleans. By twenty-two, he ran a small store and studied law. He lost an election and his store failed. In 1833, he did odd jobs just to survive. Fate never handed him any chance on a silver platter. But this kind, patient, cheerful man, with a logical and fair mind, rose in times of crisis to become "the man of the hour." When he died a martyr, the nation mourned its greatest citizen.

Lincoln never had formal academic training but possessed deep intuitive wisdom. He said his "education was picked up bit by bit under pressure."

His wisdom came from the universal spirit of life—it could not be measured by schools. It gave him strength, clear judgment, and the courage to act. With "Malice toward none; with charity for all," he suffered as a Christ-like figure once did.

True wisdom comes from the Cosmic Spirit of the universe. Knowledge is learned from the world and its authorities, but wisdom belongs to the soul.

Wisdom leads to actions that truly help humanity grow toward the perfect Cosmic Goal.

Rudyard Kipling tells a story about Tomlinson's soul standing before the gate where St. Peter holds the keys. When asked what good he had done for people, Tomlinson replied, "This I have read in a book, and that was told to me about a prince in Moscovy." St. Peter, tired and angry, said, "You have read, heard, and thought—but now tell me, by what you did with your body—what have you really done?"

Emerson said the real question is not "Is he rich?" or "Does he have certain skills?" but "Is he somebody? Does he stand for something?" Lincoln stood for something.

He was elected President because of his character and true worth. He earned success honestly, but more importantly, he used it nobly.

Chapter-9

Effort, Will, and Opportunity

Great discoveries rarely come from chance alone. This chapter shows how invention and insight arise when a trained, observant mind meets everyday events. It reveals why ordinary sights lead to extraordinary breakthroughs only for those who are mentally prepared, curious, and willing to think deeply about small things.

Many of the world's greatest inventions are often said to have happened by accident. But is it really by chance that a natural event becomes important to a mind trained by hard work and steady effort to think deeply and understand nature? For example, people say Newton got the idea of gravity because an apple fell on his head. Maybe. But apples have been falling for as long as there have been apple trees—and probably on people's heads too—long before Newton was born. What made the difference was Newton's sharp mind, trained to observe carefully and think beyond the simple fact of the falling apple to understand its cause and effect. This ability wasn't just about noticing more, but about having a well-developed connection between what his senses saw and the place in his mind where intelligence works.

The steam engine idea is said to have come to Watt as he watched a tea-kettle simmering. But thousands of people before him had seen steam rise from kettles. Galileo's idea of the pendulum for measuring time came from watching a swinging lantern in Pisa's cathedral, yet many others had seen swinging lanterns before him. What made these discoveries special was that these men were prepared to notice something unusual and then think deeply about it until they found a law or made a new idea complete.

Most great discoveries come from careful attention to small things. Printing started with rough marks made on beech tree bark to amuse children. Galileo got the idea of the telescope by watching children play with lenses. Galvani noticed a frog's leg twitch near certain metals and this led to the invention of the electric telegraph. Young studied light's behavior after observing the colors in soap bubbles blown by a child. Samuel Brown got the idea of a suspension bridge by looking at a spider's web covered with dew.

A boy once invented a way to make a steam engine work automatically so he could have more time to play. Newcomen's early steam engine needed a person to open and close taps to control steam and cooling water. This boy tied cords to the taps and connected them to the engine's beam, so the engine could work by itself.

Many discoveries came while people were looking for something else. Old alchemists, searching for gold, found gunpowder, porcelain, medicines, and natural laws instead. Goethe pointed out that many great men, like Saul in the Bible, found unexpected kingdoms while searching for something else.

Eli Whitney went to Savannah to be a schoolteacher but met a plantation owner who needed a machine to separate cotton seeds from cotton. Whitney's saw-gin, with iron teeth, could do the work of fifty men a day and started a new era of wealth in the South. Whitney couldn't find a teaching job but invented something that changed history.

Michelangelo became a sculptor after seeing a man shaping clay in a garden. Roger Bacon, trained for the church, realized that much "knowledge" was just false ideas passed down by tradition. He studied Arab scientists, criticized European science, and was accused of witchcraft. He was punished and imprisoned but became the greatest experimental scientist of the Middle Ages.

Socrates worked as a craftsman, soldier, and statesman but became the greatest ancient philosopher teaching in Athens' marketplace. Emerson called him the "Aesop of the mob," and Xenophon said you'd find him wherever the crowds gathered.

It's wrong to think people are born fit for only one job. If that were true, most people would fail unless they got into their perfect job early. In fact, once someone settles in one job and becomes good at it, much of their brain stops working in other areas. So many adults can only think clearly about one kind of work, just like skilled workers can only do their specific trade.

Henry Sherin said thousands of people live on charity or family help because they had to quit their jobs due to health or economic troubles. He saw highly educated people—professors, priests, doctors, and lawyers—unable to work outside their fields because they focused only on one subject. They got stuck in a mental and physical rut early and became unable to do anything else.

This shows the importance of mental flexibility, effort, and the will to keep learning and adapting, which open the doors to new opportunities throughout life.

Many men may not start life in the business or job they want. Sometimes, they find out through experience that the work they thought suited them doesn't really fit their nature or talents. Think of great people like Carnegie, who began as a weaver boy; Lincoln, a rail-splitter and storekeeper; Rockefeller, a commission clerk earning just four dollars a week; Andrew Johnson, a tailor; Sir William MacKenzie, who ran a small sawmill; Lord Strathcona, an Indian trader; and Edison, a newsboy on a train. Roger Williams started as a skilled cobbler before becoming a powerful preacher and champion of freedom. Moliere wasn't a successful lawyer but became a famous writer; Goldsmith was a poor doctor but made a lasting name as a great author.

Henry Clay, known for his powerful speeches, came from a poor family and was "the mill-boy of the slashes." Benjamin Franklin was meant for the ministry but never entered it. He worked as a soap-maker and printer before making his famous experiments with electricity. When people doubted the use of his work, he wisely said, "What's the use of a boy? He may grow into a man."

Great men have never been stopped by failure or by starting in jobs that didn't seem perfect for them. Macaulay said, "The world often admires not the man who does something nobody else tries, but the man who does best what many do well." Failure happens when a person is not true to their best knowledge and potential. Madison C. Peters urged, "Light your ambition. Make things happen instead of waiting for them to happen to you. If you wait to be appreciated, you'll be left behind." A spirit that does not aim high is destined to remain low. High ideals and a strong purpose, combined with willpower and energy, can lift a person from routine dullness to great success and service in the world.

Longfellow called this "the divine madness of noble minds"—the madness that never fades, but works and waits until it finds or creates what it seeks.

Genius overcomes obstacles and turns closed doors into open gates of opportunity. Lincoln had no easy chance to study law, but he walked forty-four miles to borrow important law books and read a hundred pages on the way home. Bunyan wrote "Pilgrim's Progress" on paper used to cork milk bottles while in prison. Cervantes wrote part of "Don Quixote" on scraps of leather while imprisoned for debt. England's Chief Justice Lord Eldon was so poor he borrowed and copied law books. Many great people like Fawcett, Herreshoff, Handel, Milton, Robert Louis Stevenson, Mozart, Beethoven, Carlyle, Faraday, Darwin, Spencer, and Heine all faced illness or disability but still made a lasting impact. Most successful men begin by taking the first reasonable opportunity and giving their best to whatever job they have. Every experience teaches something, and even a dull or lowly job can feed a curious mind with useful lessons. Sometimes, learning what *not* to do is just as valuable as learning what to do. Sherin noted that few bank presidents start in banks, and many railway leaders began as laborers. All of them learned through honest, hard work that built their bodies, trained their minds, and shaped their characters for greater duties ahead.

Doing a task well brings some success. Doing it better brings more. But doing it best, no matter how small the job, brings true success. Emerson said a man who makes better rat traps than anyone else will find a clear path to his door. He also said, "The greatest fortune is to be born into work that brings both employment and happiness—whether making baskets, swords, canals, statues, or songs." If a man isn't doing work that makes him happy, it's not fate or stars to blame if he doesn't wake up, clear his mind, and find a field where his talents can grow and serve others. Beethoven's motto was, "No barrier is set that can say to eager talent and hard work, 'Stop here.'"

Many fail because they don't see opportunities nearby, spending their lives chasing big things far away that turn out to be small. A California farmer sold his farm cheaply to go search for gold, only to die in the attempt—while his own land held gold-rich streams. A Pennsylvania farmer sold his land to chase oil in Canada, missing the fact that his farm's creek was polluted with oil from nearby wells. He failed far away, but his farm is now one of the richest oil lands in the country.

Wanderlust—the urge to roam—can help produce pioneers who explore new lands, but it can also lead to aimlessness, lack of focus, and failure. Lowell said, "Every man is born with his business or profession inside him," and it takes courage and determination to change your work or place to find where you can do your life's true work. "To the work we love, we rise early and go with joy." Doing work we are good at and love brings happiness and success.

No power on earth can separate a determined person from their work, and "Nobody can cheat you out of ultimate success but yourself." Daniel Webster's father wanted him to be a farmer, but Webster gave up the scythe in frustration. He was determined to get an education and become a lawyer. When people warned him that the legal profession was full, he replied, "That may be in numbers, but there's always room at the top." He worked hard to reach his goal but was so poor during his early years that when a friend sent him some grease for his boots, he laughed and said, "My boots need more than grease to keep out water—they even let in gravel stones."

John Adams's father wanted him to be a shoemaker. Ole Bull was beaten by his father for playing the violin but kept playing. True genius in a child cannot be stopped by being called "wrong" or by punishment. Schiller loved poetry but was forced by his father to study surgery. He was unhappy and not suited to it. As people say, making Schiller a surgeon was like using a razor as a chisel.

Joshua Reynolds, one of the founders of the British Royal Academy, faced his father's anger because he refused to follow his father's wishes. When his father found Joshua drawing, he angrily scribbled over the picture and wrote, "Done by Joshua, out of pure idleness." Yet Reynolds believed that hard work and purpose could achieve excellence, even in art. What some call "idleness" can actually be true work, while much that the world calls work is really idleness or worse.

Hard work is as necessary for success as genius. It's hard to separate energetic, self-sacrificing effort from inspiration. True work is driven by enthusiasm—the spark of the divine within us. George Eliot, known for her great care in writing, read over a thousand books and spent years of hard work to produce "Daniel Deronda." The famous astronomer Maria Mitchell said at the end of her career, "I was born with only ordinary ability but extraordinary persistence." Goethe, known for his wisdom and hard work, said about one of his poems, "Years of thought went into it, and I tried four times before it was right."

Leonardo da Vinci, the greatest all-around genius, spent ten years studying horse anatomy to create a statue and four years painting the Mona Lisa's face. Michael Angelo studied human anatomy for twelve years and worked seven years painting the Sistine Chapel, refusing all social invitations, saying, "Art is a jealous mistress; she demands the whole man." Giardine said he practiced the violin twelve hours a day for twenty years before feeling he could truly play.

Gibbon spent twenty years writing "The Decline and Fall of the Roman Empire." Macaulay wrote his best essays three times. Hume worked thirteen hours a day for thirteen years to complete his "History of England." Adam Smith took seventeen years to finish "The Wealth of Nations," and Webster spent thirty-six years on his dictionary. Bryant rewrote "Thanatopsis" about a hundred times, and Plato rewrote parts of "The Republic" nine times. Dickens said he had to practice reading aloud two times a day for six months before he could perform his works well in public.

Determination and hard work can break down even the toughest barriers. Demosthenes, mocked as a stutterer, practiced speaking by putting pebbles in his mouth, shouting at the sea, and talking to himself in a mirror until he became the greatest speaker of his time.

It is noble to do your best, to treat every important task as if it were your masterpiece. An old sculptor, praised for his finely detailed work, said simply, "The gods will see." Edward Everett Hale wisely said, "The sure way to success in any field is proper education, hard study to learn the art, and constant practice." Work, dedication, focus, thoroughness, and energetic enthusiasm defeat failure and guarantee success in any honest effort.

Chapter-10

Life as a Struggle for Self and Service

Life is more than earning, surviving, or repeating daily routines. This chapter explores what it means to live fully—with purpose, imagination, and inner growth. It shows how true living comes from developing the mind and spirit, choosing meaningful work, and aligning personal effort with a higher goal that gives dignity, joy, and lasting value to life.

Life is a constant struggle to discover and become your true self. A successful life uses your strengths and makes the best of your chances, all in harmony with the greater Cosmic purpose. As Hippocrates said, "Life is short, art is long, opportunity fleeting, experiment uncertain, and judgment difficult." Simply making a living does not mean truly living. Making a living is just a way to live, but the most important thing in life is to learn how to live well. Life truly ends when the growth of mind and spirit stops—even if the body keeps going. Living is not just "staying above the ground." It is not just breathing or moving. A person can breathe, move, and use their senses, yet live a tired, empty life—just "tapping, tapping upon the cold brown earth," as Chaucer described it. A man might work hard in business or in a factory, but if his mind and soul are untouched by higher purpose, his life will be no more than that tired tapping.

Life is what we make it. Our value to the world is measured by how much soul, social purpose, and energy we put into it, used in the right way. Without imagination, vision, ideals, a Cosmic goal, hope, or guiding intuition, we are dead inside. If we work only for money or material things, we are slaves to those things, getting just enough to keep working more. But if we work with spirit and imagination, we join with God's purpose and the great Cosmic forces of progress.

Life should mean much more than just food, clothes, and shelter. It should be about growing your inner self, developing your mind and spirit to help the world, and moving steadily toward a meaningful goal. Every person should have a vocation—a calling or trade—that contributes something to the world. A vocation is a person's work, the necessary activity that provides what we need to live. But work should mean more than just this—it should never be done like a machine or animal.

Many people work like machines: they start up in the morning and run down at night, acting without thinking. Holmes compared a man's brain to a 70-year-old clock, ticking monotonously through life. Life for such people is dull and joyless. Dickens' character Mantalini said about his life, "I am turning, I am perpetually turning, like a damned old horse in a damned mill. My life is one damned horrid grind." Life is ordinary and boring for such human machines. But life is not meant to be drudgery or endless, soulless routine. Life is a glory, a dignity, and a great opportunity.

Man cannot be a machine. Machines have no responsibility, but humans do. We are free and responsible, able to choose what we will do. Unless a man feels his work is meaningful, he cannot truly live. Even the simplest job can be made noble by vision and the spirit of service. Charles Ferguson said, "What makes man different from beasts is that he can, by conscious effort, improve his place in the world. Man is a worker, a creator of value, a builder of the world; he alone can imagine things that don't yet exist and, with patience, make them real. To take the world as it is and leave it unchanged is brutal. A man is truly a man only because he creates wealth and makes life better."

True culture, balance, and sanity come from work done with a spirit of service. Griggs said, "Work is worth exactly the measure of manhood or womanhood put into it—never more and thankfully, never less." He also said that some men settle into their routine and dig deeper into their daily habits until they lose the ability to see beyond them. Others, in the same job, keep growing and finding new meaning in their daily work.

A person's usefulness in life is not limited to what they do at work. Everyone can have hobbies or interests outside their job—called avocations—which use their free time. How we use our free time plays a big role in whether we succeed or fail in life. Surprisingly, the most useless lives are often those who claim to have no free time, no margin for learning new things or developing talents. These routine workers say they are too busy to improve themselves, to broaden their interests, or to grow.

True workers do find time. Even if they work longer hours than others, they make time for what their spirit needs and wants to express. The cure for a life overloaded with boring routine is more work—different, interesting, and meaningful work. The stress of a richer mental life is less than the dullness of a narrow, restricted existence. There's an old legend about a man who climbed high into the mountains to ask the gods what reward comes for all life's pain, struggles, and hard work. The gods answered, "The Labor of Life." But the man thought it was just an echo and went back down, unhappy and unsatisfied.

Whittier said, "Take from our lives the strain and stress." Shouldn't we cast away the thoughts that bring weariness, failure, and defeat? Shouldn't we develop interests that open our eyes to see, our ears to hear, and allow the Cosmic Forces to flow freely to our soul's deepest senses?

The Puritans and old ascetics believed that duty must be hard and unpleasant to be virtuous. They thought the harder and more bitter the task, the more valuable it was—like a bitter herb curing disease. But true duty is not about doing what is hateful; it is about doing what is hard, but also what we love.

There is a universal law of individuality as well as a law of growth and achievement. A real person knows themselves and understands their true inner powers.

A true person understands themselves, sets clear goals that match their strengths, and pursues those goals with steady determination. The greatest duty in life is to express your unique personality to the world. True happiness comes from developing and showing your real, inner self.

Real success means consistently aiming at the center of your purpose and refusing to get stuck in the dull routine of life. The real challenge is to learn the true art of living—gaining inner wisdom, understanding what really matters, and working toward worthy goals. "To overcome care with joy, and grief with laughter, To cherish the present without worrying about the future, To watch the sun set without regret, And greet its rise with hope—forgetting the night, To have enough to give—and find joy in giving, To feel alive and respond to every good in life—that's true living."

What matters most in life is your attitude toward your work. No matter how simple your job may be, if you do it with devotion and seriousness, you fulfill your true purpose. Ruskin said it doesn't matter whether you paint a single rose petal or a huge cliff, as long as love and respect guide your work. It doesn't matter if you spend months on a small part of your painting or finish a palace in a day. What counts is that you fill your heart with patience or push your hand with speed, always with a solemn purpose. The most important thing in work is respect for the task and putting your whole being into doing it—not just well, but as perfectly as humanly possible.

Genius is finding endless joy in your work. Genius means immortality, because a person becomes immortal through the work they love. Only work done with great pleasure keeps its value forever. Man's mission is not to try impossible tasks or waste time on problems beyond his reach. Instead, it is to discover what he can do and do it well. To educate himself fully, develop his personality, and use his talents within his limits. Happiness comes to anyone who finds work they love, and religion fills the soul of those who love their work.

A person's duty to the world, to God, and to others is to bring life and energy to their surroundings. Use all your talents and skills, and carve your message and personality with enthusiasm and strength into the world around you. Four hundred years ago, Michael Angelo wrote:

"The cold, unshaped stone Becomes a living form. The more the marble wears away, The larger grows the statue."

If a person is free to fully express their soul, their work will shine and grow. The more of yourself you put into your work—your devotion and energy—the more your inner self develops, finds happiness, and feels fulfilled. A true worker is like Pygmalion, whose statue the gods breathe life into.

Man was made not only to be active and useful but also to develop all his talents in harmony with the Cosmic Spirit of progress. Man is meant to grow and never to stand still. To succeed, you need method, patience, and focus—but you must also know when to rest your mind. Griggs said, "Endless effort is just average work, avoiding effort is fooling yourself, but the right balance of effort is the key to genius. Push yourself hard, then relax and open your mind and heart—that's the secret to great living. Either alone leads to failure."

During the day, the mind should be active because that is its nature. It should be used and directed well. Changing your thoughts brings rest, and this kind of rest or relaxation can actually help your productivity. Hobbies and interests outside work can refresh the parts of your brain tired from concentrated effort. The mind also needs time for reflection and thought—if it has the ability—because this is a sign of true culture. But it's dangerous to think too much without opening your soul to the light of truth and understanding the real world. A mind lost in dark thoughts is like a blind mole digging underground.

Many great writers, poets, scientists, artists, chemists, engineers, and inventors used their "margin of time"—spare and free moments—to create their best work instead of wasting those moments. William Cullen Bryant, one of America's earliest poets, earned his living working at a newspaper desk in New York. But the poetry he is remembered for was written during the free moments most people waste. John Stuart Mill, the English philosopher and economist, worked six days a week for 35 years as a clerk at the East India Company in London. His great literary work was done during those spare moments others threw away or tried to ignore. Matthew Arnold, the famous English poet and critic, worked in the British Government's Education Department as a school inspector from 1851 to 1886. His writing was an avocation—something he did during the rare free time he had from demanding public work.

Sir Thomas Browne lived a busy life as a provincial doctor in Britain. Yet, in his free time, he turned to writing. His first book was even printed without his permission, but it is said, "there is no English prose writer whose name is more surely remembered than his." Charles Lamb, a famous essayist, worked all day at a counting house, moving numbers from one ledger to another. But in his spare time, his warm personality and deep understanding of people shone through his writings. Lamb once said, "I can't hate a fellow I know," showing his true kindness and humanity.

William Wordsworth worked for the government and lived with his sister on just $7.50 a week. He often said that those tough years of poverty, when he had to live very simply, were some of the happiest and healthiest times in his life. Nathaniel Hawthorne worked as a customs inspector; Balzac struggled as a publisher, and Oliver Wendell Holmes was a doctor.

Nicolaus Copernicus, born to a poor baker, was a devoted Polish doctor who was always on call. Still, he found time to develop a new system of astronomy that changed how humans see the universe. He "made a hole in the walls of his simple home to watch the stars," keeping his discoveries secret for years to avoid danger. Benjamin Huntsman, inventor of cast steel, started as a poor English watchmaker. John Locke, founder of English Sensationalism and Relativity philosophy, studied medicine but was not a professional doctor. Heinrich Schliemann, the famous archaeologist, sold sauerkraut and herring in a small German village. Using his spare moments wisely, by age forty he was a skilled linguist and later left business to follow his scientific passions. Sir John Lubbock became one of the world's top experts on prehistoric archaeology by using his free time, even while managing demanding business work.

Many great discoveries in physics were made by men busy with their regular jobs but who used their "margin of time" to work on immortal ideas. Robert Mayer, who discovered the law of energy conservation, was a doctor; Carnot, the father of thermodynamics, was an engineer; Joule, who measured heat's mechanical equivalent, was a brewer; and Joseph Priestley, a theologian and philosopher, discovered oxygen. Photography advanced more thanks to passionate amateurs than trained specialists. The Industrial Revolution was driven by men who used their free time with enthusiasm and vision.

Herbert Spencer said that England's success in education came from learning "in nooks and corners," and could have added, "in spare moments by candlelight."

To waste time is to waste opportunity. Everyone has the same daily gift from the universe: 24 hours. Time is the raw material of life. Like money, its value is not in saving but in spending it well—on things that bring the best return. How are you spending your time? We save time only by using it well. The way we use our free moments shows the direction of our mind and soul and reveals our true ideals. The person who lives fully thinks clearly. Life is measured by depth, intensity, and meaning—by how well we use hours, days, and years—not by how long they last. Dante said, "The more one knows, the more the loss of time hurts."

A life is noble or not depending on the spirit behind it—not on the job someone has or their wealth or fame. It depends on how fully they use their talents and opportunities. Time is precious; ignoring chances to serve or grow is as serious as letting natural powers waste away.

"Life is too short to waste. 'Twill soon be dark Up! Mind thine own aim, and God speed the mark!" —Emerson

We truly become what we decide to be. A life without meaningful work, useful interests, and well-used time is wasted. Ruskin said such a life is a guilt that punishes itself. Yet most people drift, like machines, spending hours just to earn money while wasting golden chances to serve the world and grow their minds in their free time. Even at work, time could be made richer and more valuable by imagination, ideals, and purpose.

There is no limit to the opportunities a growing, alert person of clear thought and vision can find. But to most workers earning wages, life is a dull journey of routine, with days fading one by one into nothingness.

Seneca, the Roman philosopher, once said, "We all complain that time is short, yet we have more time than we know what to do with. We spend our lives either doing nothing, doing things without purpose, or avoiding what we really should do. We always say our days are few, but we live as if they will never end."

Some people truly live, while others simply exist. Living a life full of meaning is worth far more to the world than simply living a long time without purpose. Many of the greatest people in history had short lives, but their impact was huge. A modern teacher wisely said that spending two hours on a task means little—what matters is how much focused energy and thought you put into those two hours.

People differ not just in how long they live, but in how deeply and fully they live. This intensity of life is much more important for real progress and achievement than simply living many years. A true person would rather live one full year than waste a hundred years in emptiness.

Everyone is born with unique talents and abilities—these are their starting capital in life. The river of time flows on, never stopping, whether we use it well or waste it. "Only while the water of today's life flows over the mill-wheel can we use it. Once gone, it is lost forever in the vast sea of eternity." Every day and every hour gives us chances, big or small, to use and grow our talents, power, and character.

Goethe said, "Don't wait for great opportunities to do good. Use the common moments."Gladstone added, "Using time wisely will reward you later with profits beyond your wildest dreams; wasting time will shrink your mind and spirit beyond what you can imagine."

Nature does not like everything to be the same, just as it dislikes empty spaces. She honors individuality and refuses to make everyone equal. Progress happens because life encourages differences. Natural talents, hard work, and good use of time all matter for making a real impact on the world.

If two men have the same intelligence and energy, but one works twelve hours a day and the other eight, they are no longer equal in their effect on the world. If both work ten hours a day but one spends two or three extra hours on interesting hobbies or learning, that person's power and value will grow much faster. This extra mental work in different areas will also improve his main job skills. He will move ahead of his colleague who thinks only about work and rest, spending free time in mindless ways that only dull the mind instead of resting it.

Knowing how to organize and balance the duties and chances in each day is an important skill. We should learn to tell what is really important from what is less so, and what deserves first attention versus what can wait, for a balanced and effective life. We rightly criticize Pietro Medici for asking Michael Angelo to make a statue out of snow—a waste of a great artist's talent. Yet, we often forget that if Angelo's time was precious to the world, so is our own time precious to ourselves and meant to be used for something valuable. Are we spending our time carving solid granite—building something lasting and strong—or are we just shaping statues of snow or mud idols that quickly melt away and mean nothing?

Chapter-11

Work, Challenges, and Building Character

Life is raw material, and each person is its architect. This chapter explains how inner power, not environment, shapes character, success, and happiness. It shows why meaningful work, steady effort, and wise use of energy turn life into something strong, beautiful, and lasting—while idleness and haste slowly drain the spirit.

Goethe once said that life is like a huge quarry waiting for an architect. The architect's job is to take this rough, random mass and skillfully shape it into something strong, useful, and beautiful—a design that comes from his own spirit. Everything outside of us is just raw material, but inside us is a creative power that can turn these materials into what they are meant to be. Thomas said, "The force that drives a person toward their goals is personal power. It's the divine part of us that gives us control over the world and over ourselves. It's more than intelligence because it helps us use intelligence wisely. It's more than character because it actually creates character. It's more than personality because personality is just the expression of the mind."

Our environment does not create who we are, but it can either slow down or encourage our growth. Usually, the less support the environment gives, the stronger a person's ability to think and work deeply becomes—though this also depends on how a person relates to their surroundings. Environment is like the wind and tide for a sailing ship. Rough winds don't stop progress; they require the sailor to use skill and power to steer through the headwinds or catch the fair breeze. The environment sets conditions, but only a person can choose how to act, adapt, and strive. To succeed means using your personal power fully. Aristotle said something like this when he said, "To be happy means to be self-sufficient"—not selfish, but connected to the great Cosmic Spirit of life, which many call God.

The happiest people in the world are those who keep busy with meaningful work. Bishop Cumberland once said, "It is better to wear out than to rust out." You can achieve great things by working constantly, but the mind also needs a change of focus to stay fresh and strong. Moving from one task to another, especially when the new task excites and challenges you, refreshes the mind. Rest doesn't mean stopping completely.

One of Goethe's wise sayings was, "Work without hurry and without stopping," but "rest" doesn't mean what we usually think. Americans especially need to follow Goethe's advice: work hard and well without rushing, fussing, or stressing, because that kind of nervous hurry just wastes energy and time needed to recover.

As a poem says:
"Haste not, let no thoughtless deed
Mar for aye the spirit's speed;
Ponder well, and know the right,
Onward then, and know thy might;
Haste not, years can ne'er atone
For one reckless action done.
Rest not, Life is sweeping by,
Go and dare, before you die;

Something mighty and sublime
Leave behind to conquer time;
Glorious 'tis to live for aye,
When these forms have pass'd away."

Mental laziness is not rest. In fact, it can make you more tired than working. The old Romans said, "It's hard to rest if you do nothing." The truly unhappy people are never the busy workers or the struggling poor; they are the bored, tired, and unmotivated ones who avoid work and waste their lives trying to escape their own unhappiness.

Griggs said, "If you take from society but don't give back at least as much, you fail basic honesty and should be seen as a beggar or thief, no matter how much money you have."

Pessimists are usually sick, immature, unbalanced, or uninformed. The young pessimist, if healthy and living a full life, usually grows out of it. All the world's pessimists who had brains either died young or became more hopeful later. The busy and poor tend to be optimistic; the idle rich grow bored and fall into despair. No great pessimist has ever had to earn a living by honest work with their own hands.

Work connects us deeply with the fair and steady laws of nature and helps us believe in the order and sanity of the universe. John Wesley often told his followers, "Never be unemployed, never be carelessly employed, never waste time."

Work creates a real nobility in life. You've probably heard about the "dignity of labor" from those who sometimes use it to exploit workers. But labor itself is not dignified—work only gains dignity when it is done with thought and care, using the mind, becoming truly useful in the Cosmic plan.

William Gray, who rose from humble beginnings to wealth and respect, once scolded a worker for poor work. The worker replied bitterly, "Don't act so high and mighty; I remember when you were only Billy Gray, a poor fiddler." Gray answered, "You speak both truth and falsehood. I was a poor fiddler, yes, but I played well. I never did poor work with my fiddle. That's why I have greater responsibility now, and I hate poor work in any form." Here was a man who earned true respect by doing every small task as if he were an artist. Good work wins respect and success. Work done half-heartedly is never good work; it's dishonest labor, a kind of stealing. Those who avoid work are thieves doomed to fail and trapped in endless, miserable toil. Cervantes said it well: "Every man is the son of his own works."

Fighting against the downward pull of a wasted life and struggling to overcome the obstacles on the path to progress are what build character and lead to success. It takes a strong hero, like Siegfried, to triumph over the fierce flames surrounding Brunhilda. It takes courage and passion to overcome the hidden, often overwhelming challenges that fate seems to place before us. The world moves forward because individuals fight and rise up—not because a few self-appointed leaders lift everyone up. Every person must grow and save themselves through their own efforts.

Opportunity offers a chance, but it's rarely an easy, open path. It is more like a timely moment to fight, jump over a barrier, and face challenges boldly, with the hope of winning if the struggle is fought well. No life worth living or serving the world is like a train riding smoothly on level tracks, directed by invisible hands that control every switch. Life demands more than just sitting in the locomotive cab, watching signals, and running the engine.

Each person is like a center from which many paths spread out. The uphill paths lead to useful service, the flat ones lead to boring mediocrity, and the downhill paths lead to oblivion. Most great achievements come after a hard, painful climb—a journey that requires leaving behind useless habits and heavy, unnecessary burdens.

Resistance shapes a person. Ignatius said, "A good athlete is beaten and battered but still conquers." Young people should learn that life only gives back what they put into it. Nathaniel Hawthorne, frustrated with lazy and selfish people, said, "A man deserves nothing from others beyond bread, water, and a grave unless he earns it by his strength or skill." Without resistance, there would be no true manhood. Resistance is what sets nature's laws in motion and balances forces to make life possible. If you remove resistance, you remove character, mind, and even the divine spark from a person. Humans were not made to just exist as invisible, meaningless beings; they were made to struggle, to conquer resistance, to unlock nature's secrets, and to bring the world closer to a higher ideal through courage and wisdom.

Kant gave a great example: a flying dove faces only one obstacle—the resistance of air. You might think that if the air were removed, the bird would fly easier and faster. But without air, the bird would fall immediately and could not fly at all. The very thing that resists flight is what makes flight possible. Similarly, the struggles and challenges we face build our character and power. The harder the resistance, the stronger we become. Through these struggles, we become more like God, who is both supreme courage and supreme wisdom.

The world needs strong, high-energy people who can carry great power—brave souls who would rather face death than give up, wise individuals who see defeat as sometimes a greater victory than public success. These people know that choosing what to do often takes more courage than doing it.

Our schools should focus on developing young people who are ambitious, full of energy and purpose. When they start life's race, they should show their training and determination. The world is tired of selfish, lazy, and falsely proud young people who have book knowledge but lack real wisdom. These young people are often calm and confident in their ignorance—products of a flawed education system that mistakes luxury and comfort for true progress and culture.

Young men should enter life eager and ready to race, full of restless energy, impatient to begin, and determined to lead. Individual preparation, effort, and achievement are what bring the world closer to perfection.

Obstacles and hardships draw out the energy needed to achieve greatness. You learn more from life's struggles than from its comforts. Emerson said, "Never mind the ridicule, never mind defeat; rise again, old heart, it seems to say—there is still victory for all justice." The soul's real joy is often found in the fight, not just in winning. Seneca said, "What will you gain if you do your duty bravely and generously? The doing itself is the reward." The only way to reach your ideals is through constant, determined effort. Anything worth having requires persistent and intelligent struggle.

Many great leaders would have remained unknown if they had not been pushed into fighting spirits by necessity and resistance. Epictetus said, "What do you think Hercules would have been without the lion, hydra, stag, boar, and cruel men he fought? If he had nothing to fight, he would have just wrapped himself up and slept. Without challenges, he would not have been Hercules at all. What good would his strength, endurance, and noble spirit have been if there were no difficulties to call them forth?"

Poverty has often been a strong motivator for action. This push has led many to focus their effort and become geniuses. Everyone needs some kind of strong motivation to achieve anything meaningful—whether it is personal need or the need to serve humanity. A boy born poor may be lucky because necessity pushes him to work hard. A boy born rich must have a strong soul to succeed, finding motivation in wanting to serve others and in pure love of achievement—not just to meet physical needs.

Some great men were born into wealth and luxury and still became great. But most of the truly great men who have left a lasting mark on the world were born in humble homes and faced the full hardships and resistance of life's difficult climb.

Goethe once said, "It matters greatly which door we enter life through." But he wasn't talking about whether we are born in a humble home or a grand palace. Instead, he meant the true door is the worthiness we inherit from our ancestors—our character, strength of body and mind, and purity of heart. Wealth, social status, and flashy appearances are all superficial and don't last. A person's true inheritance is their mind and heart, their individuality, their ability to connect with others, and their physical health—whether strong and vigorous from good ancestry and living by nature's laws, or weak and fragile because of inherited weaknesses or the breaking of these universal laws, either knowingly or through ignorance.

The struggles of men and women to survive and raise their families have produced strong, healthy bodies with powerful nervous systems—and therefore brilliant minds—ready to serve the world. These minds only need the right guidance to unlock their full energy and freedom, which can amaze the world. On the other hand, the easy, quiet life of the rich and idle leads to weak bodies and damaged nervous systems. These people often become restless, addicted, or simply bored, and their children inherit nervous weaknesses. No brain formed from sick nerves can be great—just as a weak, sickly body can never compete with a strong athlete at the Olympic Games.

Life is not a game of chance where success or failure depends on luck, like drawing a winning ticket. "Success," said Choate, "cannot be accidental. You might as well drop the Greek alphabet and expect to pick up the Iliad." Where we are born does give us certain advantages, but it also brings disadvantages that balance things out. This diversity in talents and abilities is good for humanity because it helps the world's work get done by those best suited for it.

Human progress depends on this variety of skills and talents. Everyone who works hard and dreams big will get a chance to fully use their special abilities, sooner or later. Being forced to rely on your own strength, as Benjamin Franklin said, is actually a great blessing—it makes your talents grow and your energy rise like never before. If it were impossible to succeed or fail, to rise or fall, no one would try hard, competition would end, progress would stop, and the world would sleep until individual effort returned to push it forward.

The goal of mental effort is to awaken and fully use all your natural powers through your own will. External advantages like lucky breaks or a good environment are uncertain, but true and lasting success comes from sincere personal effort. To succeed, you must commit to a life of work and refuse a life of laziness. When Dionysius the Elder was asked if he had any free time, he replied, "God forbid that should ever happen to me."

Life is serious business. Nothing truly valuable, lasting, or fulfilling comes without hard, constant work over days and years. We don't really own anything unless we have earned it through effort. "The gods sell us all good things for hard work." Spinoza said, "All noble things are as difficult as they are rare," and Griggs added, "They are rare because they are difficult." There is no royal shortcut to anything worthwhile. To understand the world, control nature, and use it for humanity's good, kings and peasants alike must follow the same cosmic laws.

The path to knowledge and achievement is the path of smart, persistent hard work. It is a "highway with no toll-gate." There's a famous story about Euclid, who was asked by Ptolemy,

King of Egypt, to teach him geometry. Euclid started with definitions and rules, but the impatient king demanded, "Must a Pharaoh learn like a common slave?" Euclid replied calmly, "There is no royal road to geometry." Knowledge isn't inherited—you earn it through effort. Character isn't given at birth—you win it through life's struggles.

Kansas has an inspiring motto: "Through difficulty to the stars." Madison Peters tells of an old crest showing a pickaxe and the words, "Either I will find a way or make one." The world needs people ready to give their lives meaning—brave enough to stand by their beliefs, even if they are unpopular or go against the crowd.

As the saying goes: "The iron will of one strong heart can make a thousand quail, A small but determined soul can turn the tide of battleAnd rally the giants who once fled."

True poverty is not just found in poor slums, but often in the rich, empty homes of the worldly wealthy. Those who have no vision, no faith, no hope, no kindness, no real feelings for humanity, and no connection with the spirit of life are the truly poor and destitute. No matter how hard they work or how much they focus, true genius never reaches down to lift such souls.

Worldly success may come with true achievement and progress for all, but what is often called success is really a cold, lonely peak of selfish greed—a life lived in error and emptiness.

Life must be met with a fighting spirit. Human excellence, whether mental or moral, is rarely easy to achieve, but much can be gained with steady, honest effort. Giving up and avoiding struggle means settling for mediocrity. It is through fighting to survive, overcoming obstacles, and striving for more that character and mental strength grow. Wordsworth beautifully describes the successful worker's spirit as a "happy warrior"—

full of energy, calm confidence, self-awareness, and well-trained reason:

"It is the generous spirit, who, when brought
Among the tasks of real life, hath wrought
Upon the plan that pleased his boyish thought;
Whose high endeavors are an inward light
That makes the path before him always bright—
Who, with a natural instinct to discern
What knowledge can perform, is diligent to learn;
Abides by this resolve, and stops not there
But makes his moral being his prime care.
He labors good on good to fix, and owes
To virtue every triumph that he knows;
Who if he rise to station of command
Rises by open means; and there will stand
On honorable terms, or else retire,
And in himself possess his own desire;
Who comprehends his trust, and to the same
Keeps faithful with a singleness of aim;
Who, not content that former worth stand fast,
Looks forward, persevering to the last,
From well to better, daily self-surpast."

Chapter-12

The Art of Living and Working in the Machine Age

> The Machine Age has reshaped human life, work, and purpose. This chapter explores how people first became servants of machines, and how true progress begins when human intelligence and skill regain control. It examines specialization, industry, and wealth, showing why modern work must serve human growth—not crush the human spirit.

The time we live in is called the Machine Age, and it's also known as the Age of Human Specialization. At first, many people were trapped as mere cogs in machines, controlled by a small group obsessed with money and wealth. That harsh stage is fading. But the Machine Age itself keeps growing and changing. Now, workers are rising above mindless, repetitive tasks. They control the machines, not the other way around. Their jobs now require thinking, skill, and care.

Machines guided by skilled workers are like horses ridden by jockeys—the rider's skill matters in the race toward success. But when machines control the workers like unstoppable beasts, they crush people's spirits, turning work into dull, hopeless drudgery that kills creativity, interest, and hope. The early days of the Machine Age, especially in Great Britain and parts of our own country, were filled with terrible suffering and unfair treatment. Machines were like monsters, and workers were their slaves. Only recently have workers begun to master machines and win back their freedom.

Since ancient times, there have been craftsmen—people with special skills chosen to make important tools and weapons like arrows, plows, and swords for their communities. For many centuries, farming and fighting were the most important roles: farmers provided food, while warriors protected and expanded their tribes or nations. The strongest fighters became rulers, while clever thinkers became priests, doctors, or prophets. Artisans and merchants were often seen as less important.

In recent centuries, there has been a fierce struggle for power between business and industry. Using machines and money, kings, nobles, and priests were overthrown or controlled. Today, industry and commerce rule like demanding gods, sometimes requiring sacrifices from people. Modern civilization depends on wealth, for wealth drives the world's business.

When war destroyed everything people gained or made, nothing lasting could be built, and there was no safety net. Specialization—the idea that people focus on one skill—started as a result of individualism. As tribes found it useful for some to focus on certain jobs, it became profitable for individuals too. Skilled men and women made valuable goods, which led to exchange and barter, and eventually money was created as a standard for trade.

Adam Smith said that a nation's wealth comes from labor, and labor measures the value of goods. That was true long ago, but today much wealth comes from land value. Population growth, industries, natural resources, and location all raise land prices, especially as inventions change the world. Still, individual skill and talent have made possible the useful mechanical, industrial, and fine arts—the ability to do one thing well.

At one time, machines seemed to threaten art and culture. The cold, greedy, and selfish parts of life appeared to be winning. Marx predicted machines would increase work hours and lower wages, which were already barely livable. But history showed the opposite: the Industrial Revolution brought progress and new opportunities.

Now, art is winning over machines, and machines are becoming tools under human control. The world's ability to work has grown enormously thanks to machines, but the art of living demands that machines serve humans, not the reverse. Early machines were often destroyed by angry mobs who saw them as evil. Mental achievements were once hidden by superstition and magic and feared by ignorant people who resisted change.

The Machine Age took some poetry from life. But it also brought the printing press, telegraphs, railroads, steamships, factories, and countless conveniences that changed the world. What was once limited to a few is now shared by many, greatly increasing chances for meaningful work and service—opportunities unthinkable a century or two ago.

Education improved with the Machine Age. Even though it was often strict and controlled, education made freedom more possible. Early industrial bosses cared little for workers, demanding long hours and low pay, much like kings and lords cared little for soldiers' lives. Yet, the printing press—just another machine—helped end many kinds of oppression: political, religious, educational, and industrial. Faster travel and communication have sped up the fight for liberty. Humanity's struggle continues against rulers who claim "divine right," self-appointed authorities, and those who exploit others through control of any kind of machine, in any field. This battle will go on until the masses become independent, thinking individuals who refuse to be controlled by outdated traditions or manipulative powers, no matter what form they take.

Man was made to be free—an individual able to use nature's forces, invent, control machines, and work with others like a well-coordinated team. We have moved beyond the Machine Age, with its focus on materialism, greed, and oppression. Now, we are entering an era of true freedom.

Just like the saying "The Sabbath was made for man, not man for the Sabbath," machines, society, government, religion, and all institutions were created to serve people—not the other way around. Diderot once shouted to the church that was choking truth, "Release your God!" Today, our call is to "Release your false gods"—those rigid beliefs in politics, religion, society, industry, commerce, and education. Instead, worship truth, use reason, be your true self, follow your inner voice, and reject the false, artificial, passive ideas that blind the spirit.

Specialization—focusing on one's unique talents—has helped humanity move closer to perfection. But true specialization means intense, focused effort, not ignoring or damaging other abilities. William James said a person's total mental strength depends on all their faculties working together. Passion and interest in a subject matter more than just pure reasoning or memory lead to real success. Even if someone's attention jumps around, if they truly care about something, they will keep returning to it and get better results than someone less passionate.

For specialization to work, deep concentration is needed. This breeds creativity, new ideas, and strong enthusiasm. Great inventions come from minds deeply focused and driven by a desire to succeed. But this doesn't mean a person should narrow themselves too much—too much focus on one thing can cause other talents to weaken and the mind to become unbalanced.

The truly brilliant and influential people are those who can use many of their natural talents well, not just one. Exercising different mental abilities actually strengthens the whole mind. Genius is often the story of hard work and persistent effort, courageously facing great challenges. George Eliot once laughed at the idea that writing comes only from inspiration, and a famous teacher said genius is the powerful result of learning to work well, freely and in harmony with truth.

Great inventions don't usually come from people isolating themselves for long periods to solve a problem alone. Although focus, determination, and self-sacrifice are important virtues, they must be balanced. Life must stay natural, or else too much of anything—even good things—can cause harm.

People often say the world moves forward on two legs: "Invention" and "Imitation." While invention is praised, imitation is often doubted. But invention depends on what came before. To truly invent, one must first learn to imitate the good work of those before and around them. Winwood Reade said, "It may seem strange, but only the imitative mind can be original; an artist must copy before he can create." A true innovator studies everything about a problem—its history and current state—before using imagination to improve on it.

Some inventors work by intuition but don't know if their ideas are really new. Many create things they think are original but have actually existed before. Intuition is powerful when combined with common sense, education, research, and hard work. Genius may be intuitive, but the more skills it can use, the greater its power and usefulness. So learning, imitation, and study are essential foundations for creativity and success.

Geniuses are not freaks—they are well-educated, well-rounded people who learn from the achievements and mistakes of others. Most great artists and inventors were first good imitators.

Mozart began by copying Bach; Beethoven learned from Mozart. Molière studied Greek playwrights before developing his own style. Goethe's remarkable mind was largely shaped by his ability to imitate; like a chameleon, he absorbed the colors of his environment and then added his own genius to create something greater.

Emulation is actually a noble form of imitation. The greatest painters, sculptors, architects, engineers, chemists, scientists, and philosophers—from the Renaissance to modern times—first learned by imitating the masters before working hard to improve, clarify, and perfect their craft. Most of these immortal men began as apprentices to the greatest older masters, then bravely carried progress a little closer to the Universal Ideal.

One great modern nation is an excellent imitator. Though young in years since the end of feudalism, its people haven't yet reached the full stage of original invention, but through careful imitation, they have already achieved great success. Another powerful nation claims to have made epoch-making inventions, but these are often just the result of imitation combined with hard work and research. Their achievements cannot truly be called genius or original mental breakthroughs. This nation absorbs knowledge from around the world, understands the paths ahead, and through persistent effort and willpower, eventually discovers new ideas and processes.

There are men who gain reputations as inventors and geniuses without ever having a truly original or world-changing idea. Their power comes more from imitation and luck than from intelligent research. True inventors are broad-minded, gifted with rare common sense. Even today, nothing amazes people more than simple, clear thinking and honest, individual effort. The greatest inventors of the industrial age say their success is simply from hard, persistent work combined with what might be called "uncommon" sense.

To have common sense, a person's mind must be free from laziness and controlled by strong willpower. Sadly, most minds today are dull and trapped, so using common sense is often seen as something extraordinary—almost like genius, a divine gift. This same power exists, in some degree, in every human brain, waiting to be used for the good of all.

Yoritomo said, "Common sense is a central sense where all impressions come together and unite in one feeling—the desire for truth." If a person truly wants truth, they will search for it with steady determination—and they will find it. What is a genius but someone who brings unchanging truth to humanity, helping lift the world closer to the great Universal Ideal?

Real success follows the laws of nature, which call for the full growth and development of the mind—both as a whole and in certain special abilities. Our newspapers and magazines often tell stories of "successful" people who have devoted their lives to one thing. But when examined closely, that one thing is usually just a way to make money. These so-called successful people may be unusually good at acquiring wealth or fighting to get ahead, but their kinder, higher qualities—their idealism, sympathy, respect, and spirituality—are often dead or ignored. As the saying goes, "What does it matter if a man gains the whole world but loses his own soul?" Specializing only in business and wealth can harden the heart, kill sympathy, destroy brotherhood, promote selfishness, and turn a man into a lifeless machine—a mere cash register. The only real salvation is the full development of both mental and spiritual parts of the mind.

We hear of men who work 15 to 18 hours a day. These men generally fall into three groups:

1. Those driven by greed or who have crushed everything noble inside them. With empty lives and no true meaning, they keep working nonstop just to avoid feeling miserable, lonely, or restless.

2. Those who temporarily lose balance, honestly trying to succeed but harming themselves by overworking. Mental effort drops when parts of the brain don't get the rest they need. The brain's "gray matter" must rest and recharge, just like muscles need rest and the body needs sleep. Stories of inventors working 18 to 20 hours a day make good publicity but are rarely true. Real brain work can't be done that long—it's simply impossible and unhealthy. Many "inventors" depend more on teams and trial-and-error experiments than on their own ideas. True scientific breakthroughs come from persistent reasoning and thought, not blind luck or endless testing. One type of inventor uses past knowledge intelligently to build new ideas—an original thinker pushing humanity forward. Another just tries many random combinations, hoping for luck. This is not true science but expensive guesswork.
3. The third group includes hard-working men with demanding jobs who still have time for other interests and hobbies that benefit themselves and the world. These men are balanced, calm, and full of sympathy. They are thoughtful, imaginative, individualistic, and spiritual—opposed to all rigid beliefs and meaningless social customs. Many great discoveries and contributions come from such men, who are the true driving force in society today.

How true is the saying that a person must learn to look down on the world and even ignore it before they can truly work in it and for it? As Carlyle said, "Every noble crown is, and on earth ever will be, a crown of thorns." The great progress the world has made is mostly because of busy, practical people who had to work hard, but kept their minds alive and their souls awake. In their rare moments of rest, great ideas were born and developed into something useful.

Think of the great men from the last century who started in obscurity, laughed at and doubted by the world, but left behind inventions and ideas that changed life forever. True imagination is the source of all great discoveries and inventions; no one can be truly great without a well-cultivated imagination. Working with others in the world, facing real problems day by day, shapes a great person, deepens their sympathy, teaches them what really matters, shows them the dangers of mental slavery, and reveals the importance of the soul.

As one said, "I go forth among men, armed with pure intent, Great work is to be done, and whether I stand or fall without a crown It matters not, so God's work be done. For I have learned to value the lightning's deedAnd not the thunder after, which men call fame."

A great person struggling in the world feels the need for culture and service. They sense the strong passion of humanity and feel the heartbeat of real life. They are part of the world, and no force—whether limiting beliefs or chains of oppression—can be unimportant to them. Yet, they are not fully of the world, for their deep spirituality and personal imagination protect them from shallow materialism.

Life is a process of growth. It moves and changes; it is not still. While we live, we grow, and growth itself is life. Plato said, "Nothing ever is, but is always becoming." If life became still and routine, it would be death. Life keeps its balance through movement; if we lose this balance, chaos will follow. We cannot have life without activity. Our moving world will never become dead routine or chaos. We must keep moving forward, growing and improving according to Universal Laws. The goal of life is the art of living it well. This demands using all our mental and physical abilities to the fullest.

As one poem says, "When I was born From all the seas of strength Fate filled a cupSaying, This is your portion, child."

It is every person's duty to take this portion given by fate, use it fully, and grow. A worthwhile life is a useful life. We perfect ourselves through work. Paul Dubois once shared with Paul, after weeks of quiet companionship without preaching, this advice: "Remember, there are two duties in this world: first, to make your personality as valuable as it can be; and second, to put it at the service of others."

Pascal said a man's usefulness is spoiled by idleness, passions, pride, and selfishness—traits of ego and laziness. But this applies only to those who pretend to know but actually don't, who are weak but boast of strength.

There are also men whose great power stays hidden because they lack confidence—in themselves, in the world, or in their God. They seem suspended, afraid to take risks, worried that failure will shame them. They remind us of Don Quixote, hanging by his wrist from a stable window, imagining a great fall—only to find he was always just a few inches from solid ground. Every positive power we have was given for us to use. Only a moral coward avoids the realities of life and delays joining the fight. The longer we wait, the more our desire fades, leading to passive indifference. Some people build castles in the air, dream about what they will do, but miss real chances because they lack confidence, energy, or prefer imagination over action. Thoreau advised such people: "Make your dreams real; build a solid foundation under your castles in the air." The world needs workers, not dreamers. We must focus on what is clearly in front of us, not just what lies dimly in the distance.

The true worker has imagination, ideals, vision, and hope. They work with energy and enthusiasm. Real work is creative work, and creativity means fulfilling ourselves. Accomplishing what is near helps us reach farther goals. Emerson said, "Hitch your wagon to a star."

A wagon is a real, solid vehicle, not something just in the clouds. Emerson knew we need both the practical and the visionary. The hand can only do what the spirit sees and what the personality truly aims for.

The reward for hard work is turning ideas into reality and dreams into definite facts. Creative work always follows a clear, thoughtful mind. There is a big difference between daydreaming and having a purpose.The dreamer waits and hopes; the person with purpose acts. Doing means overcoming obstacles, fighting passivity, and controlling negative forces inside ourselves. Action creates energy that flows back to us, giving strength for the next effort. Every great mind needs a big plan and a noble purpose. But great minds must also have vision and strong belief, turned into action. Greatness comes from what we accomplish, not just from what we hope for. It is far better to be a hardworking doer, even on a small scale, than a dreamer of huge plans who never takes action. Thoreau once wrote, "A young person gathers materials to build a bridge to the moon or a palace on earth, but a middle-aged person, after wasting much of their life, ends up building a simple woodshed." Emerson wisely added, "Better honest woodsheds than impossible dreams."

Chapter-13

The Power of Mental Flexibility and Broad Interests

True intelligence is not trapped in one narrow skill. This chapter explores why a well-rounded, versatile mind is often stronger, deeper, and more creative than strict specialization. It shows how focused thinking, broad interests, and individuality allow a person to grow in many fields without losing depth, turning learning into living power rather than empty knowledge.

Versatility today means being able to switch easily from one subject to another. This quality doesn't mean a person lacks specialization, but rather that their mind holds many strong skills and talents. Each of these can be developed enough to compete with the specialized skills of others. For example, a man who spends just one focused hour a day studying a subject might become more knowledgeable in a year than someone who has worked ten hours a day for ten years. What separates the truly wise from the foolish is intelligence, focus, deep thinking, reasoning, and individuality.

A specialist who focuses on only one thing is only partly educated; their view is narrow and their personality dull and hard to bear. Such a person is mentally unbalanced and unnatural. The brain isn't like a bookshelf where every book read simply adds a new shelf. If what you read doesn't spark new ideas or make your mind stronger and more original, it adds nothing real to your thinking—just empty words memorized. A lesson that doesn't open new doors in your mind or inspire new goals is just wasted time and a bore.

Great minds have many interests—they are many people in one. Take Hippias, the Greek thinker from the 5th century B.C., known for his skill in speaking and his knowledge in astronomy, geometry, math, language, music, history, and philosophy. He was so versatile he even made his own clothes and shoes. Pythagoras was a traveler, mathematician, astronomer, teacher, and organizer. Melissus of Samos was a philosopher, clever politician, and brave general. Flavius Arrianus, a famous Stoic philosopher, was also a wise leader, soldier, lecturer, and held important government roles—all while writing on history and military tactics, and publishing the teachings of his teacher, Epictetus.

Not long ago, a modern writer tried to prove the old saying "Jack of all trades, master of none" by criticizing Leonardo da Vinci, calling him a third or fourth-rate engineer if he lived today. But versatility does not mean being a scatterbrain, just as specialization doesn't always mean mastery. A person with a developed, well-rounded mind, clear vision, and strong purpose can be great in many fields or at least be considered an expert. Doing many things doesn't mean doing them badly. The old advice, "Let the shoemaker stick to his last," has been overused—it sounds more like selfish people trying to keep others from growing.

Paderewski, the famous pianist, didn't have to be a blacksmith. But if he could have done blacksmith work without hurting his hands, the mental challenge might have been good for him—because it is the mental effort that really matters. Leonardo da Vinci was no "Jack of all trades." He revived the wonders of science that had been forgotten for centuries. He was both an inheritor of old knowledge and a pioneer of new ideas, often working alone against great obstacles. This genius was one of the greatest painters ever, a skilled sculptor, brilliant architect, engineer, doctor, mechanic, and natural philosopher. It's said no one was gifted equally in both art and science like him.

It's doubtful our time could produce another Leonardo da Vinci. Today, appreciation for art is low, minds are too focused on money, and specialists and dogmatists control ideas. This is an age of rush, noise, and crowds, full of specialists who think for us and feed us simple, watered-down conclusions. We live in a noisy, flashy time that worships appearances, money, strict rules, and a false, unspiritual idea of God—a poor copy of the true religion of Christ and the soul. People now are like Ulysses' sailors, mistaking empty bags of wind for treasure. The wild and shallow state of modern literature, music, and entertainment shows the disorder in our inner lives. We feast on what is abnormal, even though it damages and disfigures life.

Most people today boast about civilization and progress, yet they mock the great minds of ancient Greece and Rome and the Renaissance geniuses who restored a rare, free way of thinking lost during long years of mental slavery. It's been said that to find a barbarian or savage, you just need to scratch the thin surface of the average person. This idea was known long before the terrible war that shook Christian Europe. Isn't it time to listen to Marcus Aurelius' advice: "Stop being swept around"? He called such restless people "Triflers" who waste their lives in busy activity without a true goal or clear thought. He said, "Give yourself time to learn something good."

We say the world has made great progress recently. But has it really? Or is it only an illusion of speed and the false idea that luxuries are necessities? Have we truly advanced? Is our civilization really culture? Have all these years of amazing achievements brought real peace and happiness to the world?

Michael Angelo (1475–1564) was a man of many talents. Although he claimed painting was not his main interest, his artwork on the walls and ceiling of the Sistine Chapel in Rome remains one of the greatest achievements in mural art, admired across the world for centuries. By nature, he preferred sculpture and did amazing work there. But he was also an outstanding engineer—much of the grand St. Peter's Basilica in Rome is thanks to his brilliant mind. Beyond that, he was a bronze caster, architect, soldier, philosopher, and poet. In every field he touched, his work was excellent and serves as a high example for specialists even today. Michael Angelo was a big man with big ideas. As an artist driven by perfection, he insisted on perfect detail, saying, "Trifles make perfection, and perfection is no trifle." Despite living in difficult times among unsympathetic people, he gave his best to every task.

Michael Angelo and many artists of Italy's medieval golden age worked not just for themselves but for future generations. Their lasting work stands in sharp contrast to the shallow, restless, and hurried spirit of our own time—a time obsessed with the present moment and careless about the future. Only true mental growth can save us from great failure after a period of wealth and seeming success.

Francis Bacon (1561–1626), an English philosopher, scientist, politician, and writer, was another great mind. Though he ruled England in many ways, his most important contribution was reorganizing science and restoring human control over nature. Bacon was a true lover of knowledge, a creative thinker, and a hard worker—a perfect example of a balanced life.

Philosophy is more than just the study of divine and human things; it is the search for truth and the foundation of all sciences. Great thinkers like Bacon and Descartes led the way in modern philosophy. Bacon fought against blind obedience to authority and warned against wild imagination and impractical debate.

René Descartes (1596–1650), the famous French philosopher, was physically weak but mentally brilliant and well-rounded. He made important contributions in anatomy, math, optics, and many sciences. He also loved music and nature. Due to his poor health, Descartes often spent mornings in bed, which gave him time for deep reflection. From a young age, he questioned traditions and teachers and trained his mind to be free and independent. While he rejected dogmatic truths, Descartes believed in following laws and government for the good of society.

His philosophy focused on ethical beauty and law. He saw the universe as orderly and opposed anarchy, which is chaos. Descartes' practical life rules were: obey the laws he grew up with; act promptly and wisely when needed and accept the results; seek happiness by limiting desires rather than trying to satisfy them all; and make the search for truth his life's work.

Though small and frail, Descartes cared for his body like a scientist, managing his health and habits carefully. Through the constant exercise of his mind, he lived until fifty-four. His joy was in learning and thinking. While many enjoy life, few reach Descartes' level of achievement. Every mind can grow to its fullest potential and produce results, but few have the special mind and determination that Descartes had to live a disciplined life and give the world such great gifts. People often admire the results of a great mind but tend to think it comes easily—because of talent, luck, or good opportunities. What they rarely see is the hard work, the great sacrifices, the focus on a higher purpose, the giving up of worldly pleasures, and the deep, selfless enthusiasm behind that success. A person who spends their nights playing cards or dancing and sleeps late might feel overwhelmed by their daily tasks. But someone who works the same hours, loves their family and fellow humans, and still finds time to read and learn in the early mornings or evenings is actually preparing for success. What others call luck is really the result of careful planning, effort, and the steady growth of the mind. A mind that stays still grows restless and unhappy; a flexible, open mind sees life as a whole, full of chances and meaningful goals.

Take James Watt (1736–1819), inventor of the modern steam engine. He was a delicate man who, from a young age, had to rely on himself. Watt was skilled in many areas—surveying, engineering, mechanics, instrument making, and science. He was also a talented linguist with a wide range of interests. Sir Walter Scott described him as "an alert, kind, and generous man, full of talents and ideas on every subject, always ready to help others with his knowledge." A true genius isn't a narrow-minded specialist or an arrogant, unsocial person. Instead, genius carries a creative force that is both deeply human and divine. But too much focus on specialization can lead to madness. True mental growth, fully developed, reflects the Godlike power within us.

One of the most remarkable figures of the Renaissance was Galileo Galilei (1564–1642), the Italian astronomer and philosopher. Unlike many so-called successful men today, Galileo was highly versatile. He was a scholar of Latin and Greek, a logician, musician, optician, writer, doctor, and expert in medicine. He was also a mathematician and a talented painter. His father tried to limit his broad interests but failed. Galileo earned the title "Archimedes of his time." His search for truth angered the Church so much that he was threatened with torture, persecuted, put in prison, and condemned as "suspected of heresy." He spent his final years under house arrest, almost a prisoner, yet his powerful mind never slowed.

Galileo lived to seventy-eight. His best work came when he was seventy-two, and a year later, just months before he went blind, he discovered the moon's daily and monthly movements. Despite blindness, he kept working, thinking, and sharing ideas until he died. He even explored how pendulums could be used in clocks and was teaching his students about impact theory when illness struck.

While the human body peaks early and then begins to weaken, the mind, when cared for and exercised, never grows old. But parts of the mind that are ignored or neglected weaken early, leading to a "second childhood"—an unused, undeveloped mind. Many of the greatest mental achievements have come from middle-aged or older people, just as physical feats tend to come from young adults. However, not all important work comes only with age. The idea that a person should not write or create until they are forty is foolish. It's just as wrong as saying someone over forty is useless to the world.

Many young minds have made incredible contributions: Berkeley wrote his great work at twenty-five; Hume's masterpiece was at twenty-seven; Schelling earned his master's degree at seventeen and became a philosophy professor by twenty-three. The poet Keats died at twenty-five; Novalis, the mystic, at twenty-eight; Marlowe at twenty-seven; Shelley at thirty; and Christ at thirty-three.

Youth is naturally full of energy, excitement, and a strong desire for freedom and action. “Reflection whispers to the growing man,” meaning as we grow older, experience helps us calm down, see things more clearly, and understand the bigger social picture. Young people can be impulsive and extreme, often feeling discouraged when facing challenges or errors. With age comes deeper thought, greater patience, and kindness, along with a stronger connection to truth and love in the world.

People with normal brains and average health shouldn't lose their mental sharpness even in very old age. Many have done brilliant work at eighty or ninety—great minds in weaker bodies. But usually, the brain weakens with age, mostly because it hasn't been used or exercised enough. This slow decline often starts in childhood but becomes clear much later in life, when the mind should actually be at its strongest. Thoreau sadly pointed this out, saying fewer and fewer thoughts visit a man as he grows older because his mind's "forest" has been destroyed—sold for useless ambitions or wasted on pointless things. The mature person's mind doesn't lose strength because of lack of potential but because it hasn't been cared for and trained.

Education and mental growth should last a lifetime. We feel sorry for people who had poor education as children, but we often forget how important it is to keep learning and growing in later years, which can be even more valuable.

Dr. Alfred Russell Wallace, who discovered natural selection along with Darwin, wrote his important book *Social Environment and Moral Progress* when he was ninety-one years old. Wallace was a naturalist with a loving, scientific mind—a true reformer working for all people, thinking broadly and deeply. His life shows that a well-developed mind does not weaken as the body ages. He believed life is a great and noble purpose, not something to be shuffled through aimlessly.

Benjamin Franklin (1706–1790) lived to be eighty-four and was a remarkable genius. His mind was energetic and wide-ranging, focused mostly on practical results.

Franklin was a diplomat, writer, scientist, statesman, economist, and skilled in many areas like agriculture, navigation, hygiene, journalism, music, and education. He seemed to renew everything he touched, and his sharp, clear mind influenced much of the eighteenth century. Like his contemporary Voltaire, Franklin's personality was greater than any single achievement. He was not just a thinker but a doer whose work benefited mankind in powerful ways.

Though Franklin was criticized by his peers for being an amateur or "dabbler" because the age favored specialists, his wide-ranging brain refused to be limited. His famous kite experiment proved that lightning is electrical, overturning old "friction" theories of electricity and challenging expert ideas of his day. His last public effort was to fight against slavery, and he kept his calm, brilliant mind until the end.

Goethe, called "a clear and universal man," was a poet, philosopher, statesman, scientist, and writer. He shared with Shakespeare the wisdom of the world. Carlyle called Goethe an artist in the highest, most ancient sense, saying his works carry a divine spirit. People from all walks of life—from kings to common folk—have studied Goethe's writings with respect and trust, even when they couldn't fully understand them. Goethe was hardworking and persistent. Novalis said Goethe's main rule was to finish whatever he began, no matter how hard or small the task—he would master its secrets and make the results his own.

Goethe's life was full of hard work and effort. He described himself as someone who "struggled toughly." He is a perfect example of how much of what we call genius is actually the result of tireless, persistent work. Goethe was a true poet and a master of understanding people. He wasn't just a citizen of his country, but of the whole world, and not just of his own time, but of all time. His wisdom came from careful observation, attention, reasoning, and reflection, all mixed with strong intuition. His bright mind lifted him out of youthful despair and pessimism into a "better vision" full of seriousness and beauty.

Goethe was both analytical and scientific, yet also joyful, caring, and full of faith. When he died, a famous critic said, "That worthy prince, a model in all things related to literature and the arts, has been taken from us too soon." Being versatile is often a sign of genius. Goethe showed an all-around talent combined with incredible hard work, clear vision, strong ideals, and practical sense. Most great achievers have been alive and active in many parts of their nature, showing unusual flexibility in the world's drama.

The German philosopher Leibniz was so versatile that people called him the man "with a universal mind." He was an optimist and worked as a historian, naturalist, diplomat, theologian, mathematician, politician, scholar, and philosopher.

Immanuel Kant was not only the greatest philosopher of his time but also lived a life dedicated to science. He taught logic, ethics, metaphysics, mathematics, cosmography, and geography at the University of Königsberg.

Louis Pasteur (1822–1895), the son of a French leather worker, struggled to learn and was even considered slow in chemistry during school. Yet he worked hard in his own way, following a path others thought he was unfit for. He saved the milk industry from a deadly disease and made many foods safe to eat after long storage—a big problem in his time. He discovered pasteurization, a process that saves hundreds of thousands of young lives every year. He changed surgery for the better and fought diseases once thought impossible to cure.

Madison C. Peters said, "Our country is full of people who can do many things fairly well, but too few who can do one thing supremely well." If he had said that the world has many who can do one thing well but few who excel at anything, he would be right. He also said, "Every successful person must specialize, know one thing clearly. The age of universal knowledge is gone. The true measure of a successful man today is how many things he chooses not to learn—like putting a single bullet in a gun to keep it from scattering." But this idea is wrong. The age of universal knowledge has not passed—it's still far away. It's the goal humanity is working toward, and when we reach it, we will be like gods.

True success comes from having wide interests and moving closer to greatness. Both a well-educated man and a specialist use a "single shot" in their gun. But while the specialist aims at one fixed point, the well-rounded man has a wide and deep range of targets. With skill and intelligence, he can hit many more in life's battle than the narrow-focused specialist. Someone who works only to make money is a specialist. So is someone who works only for fame, or a man who builds engines and refuses to care about anything else, believing "complete focus on one thing is necessary for success."

Peters spoke about Lord Brougham's long and versatile career, which lasted over sixty years. Brougham worked in law, literature, politics, and science—and succeeded in all. When one of Brougham's friends was asked to take on a new task, he said he had no time but added, "Go to Brougham; he has time for everything." Peters admired Brougham's tireless work ethic, saying he never wasted a moment. It was said that if Brougham had been a shoeblack, he would have worked until he became the best shoeblack in England. Peters respected hard work and criticized versatility—but in Brougham's case, and for many world-famous geniuses, hard work naturally led to versatility. You can't praise hard work and reject the results it brings.

When hard work is combined with kindness and a broad outlook, it creates specialists who also have wide interests and deep understanding. If a person is naturally talented in many areas, they might become more skilled in those fields than a so-called specialist who works only to make money and does not put half the energy, intelligence, and love into their work as a versatile genius who is deeply interested in many subjects. Gerald Stanley Lee wisely said, "Specialization can be both a strength and a weakness" – not just in mechanics or industry, but also in law, medicine, art, and biology. The real movers of the world are often those who seem to "have no time," but who manage their time so well that they always find room to follow their passions.

In business, the "big" man, who has many interests and handles huge amounts of work daily, still finds time to talk with an unimportant visitor. Meanwhile, the "small" man, lacking hardworking genius, fusses a lot but does very little. He causes chaos around him and only meets with "important" visitors. It is well known that the busiest people have the most time because they have clear goals and use their time and energy efficiently. A hardworking man with compassion and understanding will naturally become versatile. How versatile he is shows how complete and balanced he is as a person. Schiller believed that success comes from "manning your own heart"—using every part of your brain and expressing all your humanity and talents fully.

Wagner (1813–1883) is a classic example of a genius who became immortal through hard work, suffering, and struggle. He became a versatile artist—a musician, dramatic composer, poet, writer, and linguist. The one who works is the one who achieves. Sometimes, necessity pushes people to do their best, but many who lived comfortable lives still worked hard in their free time to understand more about the universe. These seekers of truth worked not just for food and shelter, but for the joy and satisfaction that mental growth brings. Carlyle said the only cure for suffering is to keep striving and doing. Franklin was right to say, "The highest worship of God lies in service to man." But to serve others well, a person must truly know themselves. This deep self-knowledge brings not just knowledge, but wisdom.

A fitting verse says:
"I sought for God,
But God eluded me.
I sought my brother,
But I found him not.
I found myself,
And, finding, found all three."

Having strong purpose and enthusiasm, even with little talent, is far better than having great talent with no purpose. But the best mental life is energy matched with talent, eagerly pushing every useful skill to grow. Too much nervous energy without enough knowledge is like a powerful engine in a full boat that just spins water without moving forward.

Our duty is to develop and shape our minds to the fullest power inherited from our ancestors, and to use the energy our bodies create for good work. Specialization is good and often necessary for progress. As knowledge grows and becomes more complex, people must study deeper to reach the limits of human understanding. But it is a mistake to think specialists must ignore all other fields. Focusing on one subject doesn't mean ignoring the rest of human knowledge. A person who works hard and is deeply interested in many areas usually becomes the best specialist, leading others to even greater achievements.

Every person should develop all their talents. You either use them or lose them. Every day and every hour brings chances to grow and serve the world. Carlyle said that every day is like a burst of music that plays throughout the day—and we can choose to make it a dance, a sad song, or a strong march. Every place a person stands has its own ideal and duty. As Carlyle said, "Here, in this difficult and limited reality where you stand right now—here or nowhere—is the ideal! Work it out, believe it, live it, and be free!"

www.ingramcontent.com/pod-product-compliance
Lightning Source LLC
LaVergne TN
LVHW100731061126
851857LV00011B/479
* 9 7 8 9 3 7 2 4 4 9 5 2 5 *